Attracting Birds to your Garden

By the Editors of Sunset Books and Sunset Magazine

Lane Books • Menlo Park, California

Foreword

If you feel that a garden is not a garden without birds in it, this is
the book for you. It tells you how to increase your garden pleasure
by taking advantage of the many benefits that birds can bring.
The early pages will acquaint you with a wide range of garden birds—
their songs, temperaments, feeding, shelter, and nesting habits.
We then introduce you to some simple yet imaginative birdhouses,
feeders, and baths. The last 41 pages contain helpful descriptions
of the plants that birds are most likely to visit.

We wish to extend special thanks, for their helpful advice and
assistance, to: Dr. Matthew F. Vessel; Dr. Howard L. Cogswell;
Bob Thompson; and Dr. Robert T. Orr. Also, for his assistance on
the bird range maps, a special thanks to Chandler S. Robbins, Fish
and Wildlife Service, United States Department of the Interior.

Coordinating Editor: Sherry Gellner

Research and Text: Cristine Russell, Philip Edinger

Special Consultants: Dr. Herbert H. Wong;
Joseph F. Williamson,
Garden Editor, Sunset Magazine

Design: John Flack, Joe Seney

Bird Illustrations: Dick Cole

Cover Photograph: Ells Marugg

Executive Editor, Sunset Books: David E. Clark

First Printing May 1974

Contents

≺―≺

SPECIAL FEATURES

≺―≺

The Popular Garden Birds

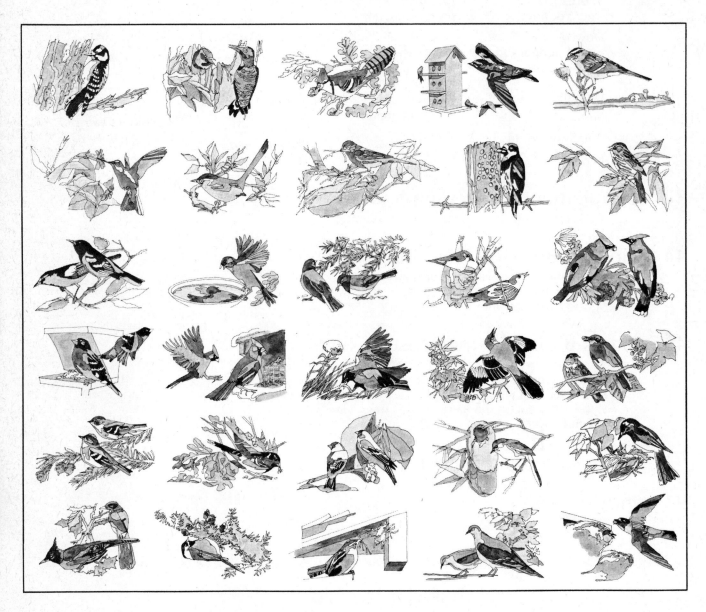

Although more than 1,500 species of birds inhabit the North American continent, don't expect all of them to appear in your garden. This number includes a variety of water birds and shy birds of the field and deep woods — all not likely to visit your garden.

A newcomer to the art of attracting birds should limit his efforts to only a few common birds. But as your interest, and the suitability of your garden accommodations increases, so should the number of birds that come to it. Some enthusiastic gardeners have encouraged more than 50 bird species — mostly songbirds — to fly into their backyard sanctuaries. Whether five or 50, bird watching can offer many hours of enjoyment.

This chapter helps acquaint you with some of the birds likely to frequent gardens across the United States. And it tells how to attract them. Individual birds are described with the gardener in mind. Look for the following information under each "bird profile."

How to attract them. Unfortunately, there is no fool-proof way to make sure birds will come to your garden. But the suggestions of favorite foods and nesting sites of individual birds offer the best means of coaxing them into your garden. Favorite food plants and choice feeder foods are included in each profile.

Appearance. There are a few tricks to recognizing each bird, and the novice bird watcher needs to learn them. Start with size. It's helpful to compare the size of a new bird with the birds you may already know.

What color is it? Some birds, like the bright red cardinal, can be easily identified. With most birds, however, you'll have to watch for markings on the head, tail, rump, wings, breast, or crown. This task becomes even more difficult when the females and young are duller in appearance than the males or when the males have different seasonal plumage.

What about shape? Is the bird's body chunky or slender? Is its bill thick enough for cracking seeds or thin so it can pick out insects from bark crevices? Is its tail long like the mockingbird's or stubby like the house wren's? Does it have a crest?

Range and migration. The geographical range varies with each species and in many cases there are counterparts on both sides of the country — in the East, the blue jay and in the West, the Steller's jay. Others — like the downy woodpecker, yellow warbler, American goldfinch, and the familiar robin — are found from coast to coast. Some birds are year-round residents; some fly south for the winter.

The thumbnail range map accompanying each profile shows you whether a bird is generally found in your area. It gives a quick summary of the bird's whereabouts in the United States and Canada at different

seasons. If a bird stays around all year, its range is shown in *dark gray*. If it migrates, the general winter range is in *light gray* and the summer (or breeding) range is in *medium gray*. This information was provided by the United States Fish and Wildlife Service. But it's only a rough guide. Remember that although a bird may be found in your area, it seeks a special type of habitat. For example, towhees need low bushy growth to rummage in, robins like the open space of a lawn, and woodpeckers need large trees for digging out insects. Therefore, the more variety in your garden vegetation, the more species you're likely to attract.

Habits. Naturally, different bird species vary in behavior. We've included nesting habits as well as miscellaneous details useful in getting to know each bird. And just by watching out the window, you'll add your own observations about each bird's lifestyle.

Relatives. Because appearances and behavior are often quite similar within a bird family, you'll also find brief notes on some related birds in each profile.

Mourning Dove

(Member of Pigeon-Dove family)

ALL YEAR
SUMMER

Noted for their tender "billing and cooing" during the spring breeding season, a pair of doves would greatly surprise the novice bird watcher if he happened to see the male jumping at the female in a mild form of aggression. However, once these mates have established their relationship, they can be seen peacefully together, searching for food on the ground or traveling together in the air.

How to attract them. In your garden, a dove may be attracted to ground feeding stations that are stocked with such choice seeds as sunflower, hemp, or millet. It will drink regularly from a backyard water source in a manner peculiar to the family of pigeons and doves. Inserting its bill into the water, it sucks the liquid up without raising its head.

Your garden can also provide favored nesting sites,

such as small deciduous and coniferous trees, as well as hedges.

Long pointed tails. Instead of hopping around like other birds, doves walk about as they feed, with their tiny heads constantly bobbing up and down. Bordered with white, their long pointed tails are excellent identification marks as they make swift, whistling flights here and there. The mourning dove's slender body is buffy brown with darker wings; the male has pinkish to bluish tints.

Nests in every state. Enjoying widespread distribution, the mourning dove thrives in farmlands, weedy fields, parks, and suburban gardens. This bird has the distinction of nesting in every state in the mainland United States, as well as in parts of Canada. But the nest it builds would win no housekeeping awards—the flimsy structure of twigs is put together so haphazardly, it's a wonder the two white eggs don't fall through. When they hatch, the young are fed a liquid diet of regurgitated milk sucked from the crops (an enlargement of the gullet or esophagus) of their parents. Before leaving the nest, they graduate to the weed seeds that form the bulk of mourning doves' diets.

Fighting birds during breeding season. The melancholy chant of "coo-ah-coo-coo" from these soft brown birds is actually the male mourning dove's love song to his mate and a challenge to other birds. Although traditional symbols of peace, the male doves are extremely aggressive during breeding season.

Pigeon relatives. The mourning dove resembles its famous relative, the PASSENGER PIGEON, a bird killed so extensively by man in the last century that it became extinct. Another member of the family is the all-too-common DOMESTIC PIGEON. It feeds on man's left-over scraps in cities and in many farmland areas.

The SPOTTED DOVE is a bit larger than the mourning dove. Its "coo-who-coo" resembles the call of the white-winged dove. It is widespread in southern California gardens, parks, and woods. Named for its large white wing patches, the WHITE-WINGED DOVE is also larger than the mourning dove. Its harsh cooing sounds are similar to crowing. This relative is widespread in southwestern states, preferring wooded areas as well as deserts. Found in Arizona and New Mexico, the INCA DOVE frequents gardens, parks, and farms. A tiny bird, it is distinguished from its relatives by its pale, scaly appearance.

Common Flicker

(Member of Woodpecker family)

ALL YEAR
SUMMER
WINTER

A member of the woodpecker family, the common flicker breaks tradition by spending much of its time on the ground instead of in the trees. Its slightly curved bill is not as effective at wood-drilling as the straight chisel-like instrument of the downy woodpecker. Instead, the flicker often tears into an anthill, lapping up the insects with a sticky tongue that can be extended more than 2 inches beyond the bill. As many as 5,000 ants have been found in one flicker's stomach.

How to attract them. An open lawn is a favorite haunt of the flicker as it hops clumsily about in search of ants. Besides insects, the flicker may seek ripe fruits and berries in season. Favorite plants include blackberries, blueberries, wild cherries, dogwoods, wild grapes, mulberries, service berries, and Virginia creepers. In winter months you can supplement flickers' natural food supply with feeder offerings of suet and peanut butter.

Like the rest of the family, flickers usually seek dead wood to carve out nesting holes, but they readily accept rustic bird boxes in the garden if entrances are

2½ inches in diameter. One to 2 inches of sawdust or wood shavings should carpet the bottom of the bird box. During winter (particularly in western states where flickers are nonmigratory), these boxes serve as roosting shelters. Ample nesting boxes sometimes discourage flickers from hammering out holes in buildings.

Splash of color under the wings. A brown barred back, a black crescent mark across the top of a spotted chest, and a flash of white on the rump as it flies about, identify the flicker. Regionally this 12 to 14-inch bird varies in coloration, formerly with two different species called the RED-SHAFTED FLICKER and the YELLOW-SHAFTED FLICKER. Salmon-red wings and tail linings gave the red-shafted flicker of the West its name. This bird has a brown crown, gray throat and cheeks, and a red moustache on the male. The more widespread yellow-shafted flicker displays brilliant golden underwings in flight. Its head markings are the opposite of the red-shaft's: the crown is gray, throat and cheeks are brown, and the male's moustache is black instead of red. Both sexes of yellow-shafts wear a red crescent on the back of the head.

Two flickers mix. Although red-shafts and yellow-shafts were once designated as separate species, scientists now commonly regard them as members of the same species, because they regularly interbreed where their ranges overlap, particularly in the Great Plains. Off-springs have interesting color combinations — orange-red wing linings or moustaches which are red on one side of the bill, black on the other. Strangely enough, young flickers resemble the father rather than the mother, as is customary. An immature female sports a moustache but loses it after the first molt.

The red-shafted flicker ranges from Alaska to Mexico and east to the Plains states. The yellow-shaft is even more widespread, ranging from Alaska across Canada south to the Gulf states. It migrates from the northern parts of its range and may winter in western states.

Comical courtship. When spring approaches the presence of flickers becomes more evident because their courtship activities are lively (and loud) performances. Courting flickers choose sounding boards such as a branch, telephone pole, tin roof, or rain spout to drum out messages, and often indulge in comical acts of bowing, dancing, nodding, or chasing one another.

Over a hundred names. The flicker's popularity throughout its wide range is ascribed to by the endless local names it has received. Colorful aliases include high-hole, golden-winged woodpecker, yellow hammer, partridge woodpecker, wake-up, yocker bird, harry wicket, and wilcrissen.

Acorn Woodpecker

(Member of Woodpecker family)

ALL YEAR

Acorns scattered on the ground and around trees and fence posts, or power poles studded with acorns are positive clues to the presence of the acorn woodpecker. Other strong clues are the raucous, harsh calls sounding like "jacob-jacob-jacob" resounding in the vicinity, and the sight of a white rump patch and two white patches (one on each of its black wings) as the bird flies by.

How to attract them. Because its predominant food supply is the acorn from native oaks, only a limited effort can be made to directly attract the acorn woodpecker to your garden. This bird will eat almonds, walnuts, cherries, peaches, apricots, and other orchard fruit. Other plants such as manzanita and madrone that provide soft fruits may lure this western woodpecker to the garden area. Insects (caught on the wing in flycatcher style) make up about 25 per cent of its menu during nesting time.

A clownish character. The acorn woodpecker can be aptly called "the clown of the woodpecker clan." Made up like a clown, it has a white face with a black chin patch, whitish eyes, and a red skull cap. Besides its appearance, the bird behaves somewhat like a clown. Whenever it flies to join a gang of other woodpecker companions in a tree, an active fluttering of wings is combined with a series of bobbing, nodding, turning, jockeying, and choruses of loud chattering.

Hammers acorns into wood. Naming the acorn woodpecker was not accidental. This bird has the curious habit of using its chisel-tipped bill to carve little holes in tree trunks and other wooden sites for acorn granaries. First it drills a hole about the size of an acorn. Then it selects an acorn barely fitting the opening and hammers the acorn into the hole. Although this may appear to be an effective way to store its food, the woodpecker does not return regularly to retrieve the acorns for food. Occasionally squirrels will try to get the acorns out but often give up in frustration. Some power poles are so heavily riddled with acorns that telephone linesmen have to regularly replace the weakened poles.

In one interesting incident, an acorn woodpecker drilled a hole under the eave of a country school house. It then attempted to fill the hole with an acorn, but the acorn fell into the space between the walls. Because the hole was not closed, the bird persistently continued to hammer acorns into the cavity one acorn after another. The children heard the sounds of the tumbling acorns for weeks. At the close of the school year, they opened up the wall to investigate. Over a thousand acorns were counted.

Favorite haunts: oak trees. Acorn woodpeckers abound in oak woods in valleys and nearby hillsides. In towns where oak trees are plentiful, this bird may also be a common resident. For a nest it makes holes in trees, preferably one that's dead or rotting. Cottonwoods, pines, sycamores, large willows, and oaks serve as nesting sites. The acorn woodpecker ranges from Oregon south to Mexico, including parts of Arizona, New Mexico, and Texas.

Conspicuous eastern cousin. The RED-HEADED WOODPECKER is draped in solid masses of contrasting red, white, and blue; its head and neck are scarlet. The snow-white wings and glossy blue-black back complete its unmistakable look. Like the acorn woodpecker, this bird stuffs nuts and acorns in holes and cracks in trees, buildings and poles. A very active, bustling, and playful bird, you'll often see it drumming or tapping various objects. Searching tree trunks for insects, the red-headed woodpecker will sally out in flycatcher style to snare insects on the wing. It will veer toward an abundant supply of beechnuts (its top ranking food choice) but will take suet also. Unlike most other woodpeckers in the family, the red-head migrates widely.

Downy Woodpecker

(Member of Woodpecker family)

■ ALL YEAR

The most familiar bird of its family, the downy woodpecker calls out its presence by pounding a tree trunk with its stout, chisel-like bill. In the mating season, this distinctive woodpecker call is especially common for attracting a mate or warning other birds not to violate its property rights. The strong bill also functions as a food gathering device. With it, the downy, like other woodpeckers, can peck here and there for burrowing insects in a tree.

How to attract them. The tiny downy woodpecker often enters suburban gardens and city parks to feed and nest. Unfortunately for this bird, tree surgeons have destroyed many potential nesting sites by removing dead tree trunks or limbs. The downy likes to chisel out a gourd-shaped nesting cavity, leaving a bed of wood chips in the bottom to cushion its four or five white eggs. With a scarcity of dead trees around, it may go to work on a telephone pole or thick fence post. You can help this situation by putting up nesting boxes in the live trees in your yard. Because these woodland birds seem to prefer a close replica of their natural nesting cavity, a rustic bark-covered box with a 1¼-inch entrance hole is the best bet (this type of box also suits nuthatches and titmice). Place the box 6 to 20 feet from the ground and line the bottom of the box with sawdust or wood chips mixed with moist earth.

The insect-devouring woodpeckers usually select a garden with large trees. Occasionally they search for food by circling up a tree trunk to the top, then they fly to the bottom of the next tree and start up again. The downy may also inspect outer tree branches for insects. A year-round resident, the downy is valuable for digging out insect eggs and larvae as well as burrowing for adult beetles and caterpillars. About one-fourth of this woodpecker's diet is vegetable, including food from cherries, dogwoods, mulberries, oaks, sumacs, and Virginia creepers.

Snacking on suet, peanut butter, nutmeats, and doughnut crumbs at the feeder, the downy may become one of your favorite winter visitors. You might leave additional suet in a container attached to a backyard tree.

Black, white, and a splash of red. The smallest of our woodpeckers, the downy measures only 6 to 7 inches in length. It has conservative black and white coloring (the male wears a red patch on its head). A white stripe extends down the back.

The downy, like other woodpeckers, is remarkably adept at traveling up tree trunks in search of hidden insects. Strong feet with two toes in front and two in back (in most backyard birds, it is a three and one combination) help woodpeckers cling to tree bark; their stiff tails serve as props. The sturdy beak powerfully cuts into the bark, and the long, barbed tongue effectively spears soft grubs. You might wonder how a woodpecker withstands the continual hammering of its bill. The answer is an unusually thick skull case that softens the blows.

A bird for all seasons. The downy resides in wooded areas almost universally across the United States and Canada and even as far north as Alaska. Likely to frequent the haunts of man rather than isolated mountain forests, the downy may be found in your garden throughout the year. In the middle of winter, the downy often searches for food in the company of chickadees, nuthatches, and titmice. In northern states the wintering downy is likely to shift southward, so the woodpeckers seen in your garden may not be the same birds seen in summer.

A larger relative. The sociable downy woodpecker keeps closer to civilization than its shyer relative, the HAIRY WOODPECKER. They're almost identical in appearance, but the 8 to 10-inch hairy is a larger version, half again as long as the downy and twice its weight. While it prefers more heavily forested regions, a hairy woodpecker may occasionally feast on suet at your feeder or even nest in a tree box.

Black Phoebe

(Member of Flycatcher family)

ALL YEAR

Perched on a fence or tree limb, an alert black phoebe will suddenly spy a fly, then sally forth, snap up the insect with a loud click of the bill, and return just as quickly to its perch to enjoy its catch. Rising at dawn, the phoebe endlessly repeats the feeding process until dusk sets in. But unlike its pugnacious relative, the EASTERN KINGBIRD, which fearlessly attacks other birds and mammals, the little phoebe is not a complete tyrant. It will peacefully keep to itself, searching for insects, and shows its aggressive nature only if another bird comes near its nest.

How to attract them. This bird of the West favors the haunts of man, nesting more often in sheltered spots under bridges, eaves of buildings, or porch ledges, rather than on cliffs in the wilds (its choice before man's settlements became available).

In rural or suburban areas, you can encourage phoebes to nest nearby by erecting nesting platforms on the sides of houses, garages, or sheds. The base of the platform (6 inches square) should be placed 8 to 12 feet above the ground. If you can't place the platform under a protecting eave, attach a sloping roof.

If your garden is near a pond or stream, the black phoebes are certain to satisfy their fascination with water by regular visits. They are welcome visitors to gardens, catching their insect prey on the wing.

A suit of black and white. The black phoebe is the only flycatcher in the United States with a black breast. The black portion of its upper body meets the white belly in an inverted V, giving an overall trim, tailored appearance. Although its coloring is similar to that of a junco, you can easily spot the bright-eyed black phoebe by its upright posture and habit of wagging its tail while perched.

A resident of the West. Unlike most other flycatchers, the black phoebe does not migrate but stays year-round from northern California to central Texas (and as far south as Argentina).

Its relative, the EASTERN PHOEBE (less handsomely colored in gray-brown and white), winters in the southeastern United States and travels north as far as Canada each spring when warm weather awakens its insect food. In perhaps the first bird-banding experiment in America by John James Audubon, a phoebe's leg was tied with a silver band. Results proved that these migrating birds return to the same nesting sites each year.

Phoebes call out their names. While differing in voice, both western and eastern phoebes seem to call out their common name with an emphatic "fee-bee" as they perch, rhythmically bobbing their tails in time to their own music.

GARDEN BRIGHTENERS: THE HUMMINGBIRDS

Noted for its unique flying ability, the delicate hummingbird hovers over flowers, thrusting its needle-sharp bill inside the blossoms to gather nectar and minute insects and spiders. This ability to hover with its body almost motionless is due to the rapid motion of its powerful wings (for its size), creating the low humming sound which gave hummingbirds their name. Darting about from flower to flower, a hummingbird seems to move in an effortless fashion. It can even fly backward when the need arises. But the constant state of animation requires an extraordinary amount of energy. The hummingbird must constantly (perhaps every 10 minutes or so) gather new food for strength. By the end of the day, it may have consumed more than half its weight in sugar.

How to attract them. Hummingbirds have formed a valuable partnership with certain flowers. The flowers attract the "hummers" (a shortened term for hummingbirds), providing a rich source of sweet nectar and an insect diet as well. As the hummer hungrily feeds, pollen from the flower brushes off on the hummer's body. When the hummer goes to another flower of the same species, the pollen is transferred.

The best lure for a hummingbird seems to be the nectar at the base of a brightly colored tubular or funnel-shaped flower. Red and orange hues seem most popular, because they stand out most sharply against the green background.

Because hummingbirds frequently feed from dawn to dusk, a garden full of their favorite flowers is sure to attract their attention. When flowers are not abundant, you can supplement the hummingbird's diet by putting out a hummingbird feeder. The National Audubon Society recommends the following mixture and preparation of food for the feeder: mix one part sugar or honey to four parts water. Stir and bring to a boil. Then add color — either by adding red food coloring or grenadine syrup to the water or by tying a red bow or artificial flower to the container. Once they discover your feeder, hummingbirds return again and again, so don't confuse them by changing location or failing to refill on time.

When hummingbirds aren't feeding, they often enjoy taking a bath. This is done simply by shaking the morning dew off wet leaves or by flying through the light spray of a sprinkler. A shallow pool of water in a flat saucer or rock may also attract them.

Iridescent splendor. Although they naturally occur only in the western hemisphere, the magnificently colored hummingbirds have gathered admirers around the world. John James Audubon fondly called them "glittering fragments of the rainbow." Unlike the diverse tropical hummingbirds (many are named after precious gems), the species in this country are adorned mostly with iridescent red-violet throat feathers and green backs. The northern hummers are all similarly small — about 3 inches long. Like other birds, the females and young are usually plainer than the brightly dressed males.

North to Alaska. Hummingbirds are more abundant in the western regions of the United States and Canada (where seven species have their breeding ranges) than in the eastern lowlands (where only one species is found). Several other Mexican species venture into southern Arizona, Texas, and New Mexico.

Most of the hummingbird species have migratory habits to some extent. They move southward for the winter and return each spring to their breeding grounds in time for the first flower blossoms. The flying strength of these birds is demonstrated by the great distances some species travel. It's believed that the eastern ruby-throated crosses the Gulf of Mexico when migrating and that the western rufous travels north to Alaska in the summer. The journeys of other species are not so ambitious.

Courtship dives. In the spring, male hummingbirds begin their courtships with great flare. They don't sing, but instead attempt dazzling aerial maneuvers — swoops, dives, loops — to woo their mates. Perhaps the most elaborate flight display is that of Anna's hummingbird. The male shoots up, almost out of view, then dives vertically down at amazing speed, finally changing direction to loop upward again. At the bottom of his circular path, he sounds a "bark" similar to that of the California ground squirrel.

After such a spectacular courtship, the male

generally lets his mate do the entire job of nest building and raising a brood. She skillfully constructs a bowl-shaped nest in a shrub or tree, usually covering it with lichen or cobwebs. Although the exact size varies by species, the nest opening is often no larger than a silver dollar. The female lays two white eggs — each only about a half-inch long—which hatch two weeks later. To feed her young, the female skillfully inserts her sharp food-filled bill into their mouths. Meanwhile, the polygamous male may take on another mate.

Except for the brief mating period, hummingbirds are usually seen alone, flying from blossom to blossom. A brief summary of the major species follows:

ALLEN'S HUMMINGBIRD. From a warm winter home in Mexico, Allen's hummingbirds migrate through southern California and Arizona to their narrow breeding range along the California coast. Although the male's brilliant red throat resembles the coloring of its relative, the rufous hummingbird, it can be distinguished by its green back. Rufous and Allen's females are indistinguishable except to the expert. The spring courtship dance of the male is dramatic: he flies back and forth like a pendulum, suddenly climbs upward for about 100 feet, then dives down in front of the female.

ANNA'S HUMMINGBIRD. Familiar to many California gardeners, this hummingbird is welcomed as a year-round resident. Unlike other western hummingbirds who shift southward during the cooler months, it stays mainly in its home area. The male Anna's is the only hummer in the United States who sports a red crown as well as a red throat. The female has a green crown. Both male and female have green backs. Of all the California hummers, Anna's is the only one with a true song. A spectacular diver (see page 10).

BLACK-CHINNED HUMMINGBIRD. This hummingbird breeds over much of the West south of British Columbia, but is most abundant in the southern portions of its range. Often found in semi-arid foothills and canyons near water, the black-chin also seeks blossom nectar in suburban communities. Although the throats of other hummingbirds may look black until the light catches their iridescent color, this species is the only one with a truly black throat, bordered with a violet band. A stark white collar below the black chin identifies the male, but the female is difficult to recognize. The black-chinned male courts his chosen mate with long pendulumlike swoops, including horizontal figure eights.

BROAD-TAILED HUMMINGBIRD. Commonly found in the Rocky Mountain region, this hummingbird ranges from eastern California, Nevada, Idaho, and Wyoming south to Mexico where it winters. With its green back and red throat, the male is similar to the ruby-throat. But it's sometimes easier to recognize the broad-tail male by its sound rather than eye: its wings produce a shrill metallic whistle as it flies. The less colorful female is easily confused with the females of other western hummingbirds. Arriving in spring, the broad-tail feeds off flower blossoms in the lower foothills. As the season progresses, it seeks blossoms at higher elevations.

COSTA'S HUMMINGBIRD. A bird of the desert and dry foothill regions of the Southwest, the Costa's hummingbird breeds from southern California east to Utah and south to Mexico. It shifts slightly southward in colder months. The male has a purple crown. This royal color continues into its unusual throat feathers which extend out at the sides. During his courtship flight, the male follows a rapid U-shaped course.

RUBY-THROATED HUMMINGBIRD. Because it's the only hummingbird seen east of the Great Plains, the ruby-throat is easy to identify. The adult male has a bright red throat; his mate's throat is white. Both have green crowns and backs. The male's tail is forked and lacks the white spots found on the outer tail feathers of female and young. Ruby-throats breed over much of the eastern lowlands, but winter south to Panama. To survive the long migratory journey, the little ruby-throat stores needed energy by gaining weight prior to its departure.

RUFOUS HUMMINGBIRD. This hummingbird travels farther north than any other hummingbird. Each spring it flies from Mexico through the lowlands of the Pacific states to its breeding grounds in the Northwest, from Oregon and Montana north to Alaska. At the end of summer, the rufous migrates south along the crests of western mountains. From every angle, the rufous male is a fiery ball of color — its back, sides, and tail are red-brown; its throat is iridescent red.

FAVORITE HUMMINGBIRD PLANTS

SHRUBS & TREES: *Abutilon, Acacia, Aesculus, Albizia, Beloperone, Buddleia, Callistemon, Cestrum nocturnum, Chaenomeles, Citrus, Cotoneaster, Eriobotrya, Eucalyptus, Fuchsia, Lantana, Liriodendron, Lonicera, Melaleuca, Melia, Poinciana, Ribes, Weigela.*

VINES, GROUND COVERS: *Arctostaphylos uva-ursi, Cotoneaster, Lonicera, Tecomaria capensis.*

PERENNIALS: *Aloe, Althaea, Aquilegia, Delphinium, Digitalis, Heuchera, Kniphofia, Impatiens, Lobelia, Mimulus, Monarda, Nicotiana, Penstemon, Phlox, Zauschneria.*

ANNUALS: *Delphinium,* Morning glory, *Salvia.*

Barn Swallow

(Member of Swallow family)

SUMMER

Swallows, migrating north by day in flocks of thousands, are traditionally welcomed as harbingers of spring. Because swallows feed almost exclusively on insects, their northern path is determined by the warm weather necessary to awaken insects. If a few swallows arrive in northern territories before spring has really settled in, a sudden cold snap can cut off the insect supply, leaving the birds hungry. Those that die in one of these late freezes give unfortunate proof to the old saying "one swallow doth not a summer make."

How to attract them. As their name suggests, barn swallows have long been thought of as residents of farming areas. They use barns as nesting sites, constructing open cups of mud and straw (lined with feathers) on the roughhewn, exposed beams inside. Modernized farming has made the old-fashioned barn with its wide, open doors a rarity, forcing the barn swallows to choose nesting sites under bridges, culverts, and under the eaves of outbuildings in semi-urban areas.

You can provide additional nesting sites for these graceful aerial birds by nailing nesting shelves horizontally under the eaves of your garage, garden shed, or house. (If the eave doesn't protect the nest from the elements, add a slanting roof to the platform.) As an added help, provide containers of mud and straw for these nest masons.

Long, pointed wings. Barn swallows spend the greater part of each day in the air catching insects. Although the swallows have small bills, their mouths are wide and open up to scoop in flies, beetles, moths, wasps, and other insects. The swallows' long, pointed wings and huge mouths are well suited to aerial maneuvers, but their feet are tiny and weak, enabling them to walk only short distances with an awkward gait.

South America to Alaska. The barn swallow was welcomed by the first settlers in America. They were able to recognize it easily by its familiar dark blue back, deeply forked tail with white spots, and rusty-orange underparts. Arriving in breeding grounds around the United States and even as far north as Alaska, barn swallows are completing a long journey from their winter homes in South America.

Young feed young. If they have happily settled in your garden for one season, swallows may faithfully return to nest in the same spot in succeeding years. They may even renovate last year's nest rather than build another one. Though both sexes help build the nest, it's the female's job to warm the eggs. Once they hatch, the parents scurry around for insects to feed the hungry young. After leaving the nest, the ability of young swallows to catch insects seems to come very rapidly. When their mother has a second set of young, members of the first brood often help feed them.

Life in the air. Besides flying around to catch insects, swallows often seem to stay in the air just for the pleasure of flying. Because of this ability to spend so much of its life on the wing, the pioneer ornithologist, Alexander Wilson, once tried to calculate just how many miles a swallow flies in a lifetime. His estimate of over 2 million miles seems overly high, but it nevertheless indicates the flying stamina of these birds.

More swallows. Relatives of the barn swallows also nest in man's dwellings. The CLIFF SWALLOW, easily distinguished from the barn swallow by its square tail, is best known as the bird who returns so dependably each year to the Mission San Juan de Capistrano in California. Many believe that it returns each year on the exact same day, but actually its arrival time varies, depending on the weather. The cliff swallow builds its jug-shaped mud nest on the faces of apartment, office, and school buildings in cities and towns, as well as under the eaves of houses, barns, archways, and bridges. In the West, it is more commonly seen nesting under bridges and on cliffs.

A common nester in tree cavities or birdhouses in open country near water is the TREE SWALLOW. Huge migrating flocks of these deep blue or green-backed birds often feed on fruits of bayberry before departing for southern wintering grounds. In the West, the VIOLET-GREEN SWALLOW nests in tree or cliff cavities and occasionally in birdhouses.

Cliff Swallow

(Member of Swallow family)

SUMMER

If you see a group of birds performing an overhead aerial exhibition of expert maneuvering, they may turn out to be a flock of cliff swallows. The swallows' pattern of gliding is as if they were riding an invisible roller-coaster in mid-air. Like other swallows, cliff swallows use their short beaks and wide mouths to catch insects as the birds fly swiftly through the air.

How to attract them. Attracting cliff swallows to your garden is not easy. If the birds are in the area and your garden has suitable structures for nest building, you may be able to draw them into it. Potential nesting sites are the rough-surfaced eaves of barns and buildings. Because swallows need mud to fashion their jug-shaped nests in the eaves, nearby mud puddles may also help to lure these birds. Although they are very dexterous in snatching mud by the mouthfuls while hovering over the mud puddle, they seem to prefer gathering the mud while standing by the edge of the source even though their weak feet do not offer a sturdy stance.

Cast of thousands. Cliff swallows are like potters and masons rolled into one. They use clay mud to build their bottle-shaped nests. An excessive amount of sand in the mud may cause the nest to fall from its niche when it has dried. Therefore, it's a dire necessity that the mud have the right amount of clay in order to give the nesting material the adhesiveness it demands. Before man-made structures were available, the swallow always nested on the sides of cliffs. In the West many of them continue to use these natural habitats. You'll see flocks of thousands nesting in a colony. In towns and cities, even a few pairs of swallows will set up their little commune under bridges, archways, and other dwellings of mankind.

Purple Martin

(Member of Swallow family)

SUMMER

As long as two and three centuries ago, the Choctaw and Chickasaw Indians in the South were hanging clusters of gourds in their villages to be used as homes by the purple martins. The martins also found homes in the cavities of cliffs, caves, and trees. Today many of these glossy black birds (largest of the swallows) are attracted to man-made "apartment houses," especially designed to meet their needs.

How to attract them. Normally, you can attract a group of martins to your garden by building a multi-roomed house to accommodate from 10 to 30 nesting pairs. Each room should have an outside entrance 2½ inches in diameter. If you want the house to be used only by martins (starlings and house sparrows also like this type of nesting site), don't locate it in your garden until the first martins arrive in the spring. Set it on a pole 15 to 20 feet high in an open area. This makes it easy for pairs of martins to come and go and enables you to watch them. If you place the house too close to yours, you'll probably be awakened early each morning by the birds' clamorous chatter.

For food, the martins will ravage the insect population in your garden, industriously gathering mosquitoes, flies, beetles, and other flying insects.

Watch them fly. These streamlined birds hunt on the wing with a graceful, gliding flight, alternating with rapid flapping of their wings. As they soar overhead, you can easily distinguish males from females. The male's color, unlike that of other North American swallows, is purple-black all over. The martin females and juveniles, however, have light underparts. On a sunny day, the head and tops of the martin's wings catch the light, flashing a purple iridescence.

Summer birds only. After wintering in South America, martins head north for their breeding grounds across the United States (but they don't nest in the Great

Basin). Their arrival time varies — from the first hardy birds in January to late stragglers in April. The males (usually the first to arrive) aggressively squabble for their chosen space. When the females arrive, mates and accommodations are chosen, and the birds get down to the business of nest building. Both sexes carry in bits of grass, leaves, twigs, feathers, paper, string, and other debris they may find.

Giant flocks. At the end of summer, the martin families, like other swallows, gather to form giant flocks for their southern journey. At night, as many as 100,000 birds have been counted in a roosting flock. Because martins have become such popular summer residents in many northern areas, bird watchers are sorry to see them move south each year. Two such examples of local devotion to purple martins are Greencastle, Pennsylvania, where colonies of martins have nested in boxes since the 1800s; and Griggsville, Illinois, which proudly calls itself the "Purple Martin Capital of the World."

Blue Jay

(Member of Jay family)

ALL YEAR

Although exceptionally handsome with unmistakable bright blue coat, white front, and black neck scarf, the well-known blue jay is known as the "bad boy" of the bird world. Many bird lovers dislike jays because of their reputations (perhaps exaggerated) as nest robbers who devour the eggs and young of other birds. Others dislike the jay because its noisy and aggressive behavior at the feeding table scares away smaller birds. Even with these faults, the blue jay retains a fan club because it provides an alarm service against potential danger for other birds. Shrill, ear-piercing calls ring out at any sign of approach, whether it's a prowling cat, feathered enemy, or human.

How to attract them. The blue jay once frequented only the eastern woodlands. Now it is commonly seen visiting suburban lawns, gardens, and city parks. Jays aren't the least bit particular about what they eat, but they have found that their search for food is easier if they stay near developed areas.

The blue jay's all-purpose stout, strong bill makes an excellent tool for cracking open the hard-shelled acorns it loves. Bracing the nuts between its feet, the jay chisels through the shell to the soft mass inside. Blue jays can open sunflower seeds placed in the feeder using this same technique. They also gorge on peanut butter, cracked corn, and suet (often carrying off large chunks unless you hang it in small mesh bags or suet logs, see page 39).

Away from the feeder, the jay's diet includes the seeds and nuts of oak, beech, and pine, and the fruits of cherry, grape, huckleberry, mulberry, and plum. About one-fourth of the jay's diet is animal, largely consisting of insects and a sampling of tree frogs, salamanders, and mice, and, in season, the eggs and young of small birds.

Displaying a bold and brash manner most of the year, the blue jay becomes cautious and secretive during the nesting season, searching for suitable nest sites in the dense growth of deciduous or evergreen trees. Oak trees are favored spots, but jays will happily settle in alder, cedar, elm, hemlock, maple, and pine. The nest is usually built close to the trunk on a limb that is at least 10 to 20 feet high. Sometimes the coarse, cup-shaped nests are located in vines that grow about porches and chimneys.

Far from melodious. Though it may seem improbable, the jay is related to the COMMON CROW. Technically, both belong to the songbird group, but the cawing of crows and the screeching of jays are far from melodious. Although blue jays are best known for their loud, raucous chatter (either singly or in groups), their repertoire includes an expert imitation of hawks and the soft notes of small birds.

Southward migration. Though many jays are year-round residents in the eastern United States, a general southward shift of the birds occurs during cooler months. After pairing off for the breeding season, jays may band together in winter to look for food. But, they seldom fly across open space as a group, preferring instead to cross from tree to tree one at a time in order to escape their predators' attention.

Jays plant oaks. The blue jay has a miserly habit of collecting nuts in the fall and storing them in various places (often beneath a few leaves on the ground) for winter food. Many are never recovered. Some of the nuts left hidden are acorns which sometimes root and sprout.

Steller's Jay and Scrub Jay

(Members of Jay family)

■ ALL YEAR

Bird novices often mistakenly call the jays they see in the West "blue jays." Actually, the true blue jay is normally a resident of the East and Midwest and will be seen ranging generally only as far west as the Rockies. Several kinds of jays roam the West, but the two most commonly seen at garden feeders or park picnic grounds are the SCRUB and STELLER'S JAYS.

How to attract them. Both jays are attracted to backyard feeders, particularly if you stock them with bread, corn, cracked nuts, peanut butter, and suet. Alike in natural feeding habits, they eat insects, nuts, fruits, and berries found in gardens. Jays are often scorned as nuisances because they also eat cultivated fruit, as well as the eggs and young of smaller birds.

Both wear blue. The scrub jay is crestless, 11 inches in length, and has blue wings, a brownish back, and a white throat. The Steller's jay is black and blue in color and stretches over a foot from tip to tail. Like the blue jay, it has a prominent crest that stands up when its curiosity is aroused.

Scrub jay likes the West. Although it may have roamed from coast to coast at one time, the scrub jay now seems to be a happily settled resident of the West (from southern Washington and Idaho and Wyoming, southeast to southern Mexico) and central Florida.

You'll rarely see it in between these two regions. While behavior varies among its various forms (once considered different species), the scrub jay readily visits feeders and often becomes tame enough to take food from your hand. Scrub jays naturally dwell in the brushy growth of hillsides, nesting most frequently in oaks, pines, junipers, hawthorns, wax myrtles, and willows. They also have adapted to urban surroundings. You'll often see one completely relaxed on a tree perch or telephone wire, its long tail drooping downward.

Steller's choose conifers. Named after George Steller, a member of the Russian expedition that discovered Alaska in 1741, the Steller's jay habitually resides in conifers, particularly pines, preferring those trees in cooler or shady areas. Breeding in the western mountains, it descends to lower elevations in the fall, commonly seeking food in backyard trays and park grounds. It may carry food up a tree, hopping upward as if it were following a spiral staircase. In the more humid coast belt of central California and northward, the Steller's jay is seen all year-round.

Both serve as sentinels. The scrub and Steller's jays, like other jays, are noisy birds. They'll attract your attention with loud shrieks that also serve as a warning to other birds of approaching danger.

Black-capped Chickadee

(Member of Chickadee-Titmice family)

ALL YEAR
WINTER

If you see a tiny gray bird with a black crown, gray back, black bib, and white cheeks hanging upside down from a limb of a pine tree, it may be a black-capped chickadee. More an acrobat than a flier, the chickadee is just as happy looking for insects under a branch as on top. These persistent pest detectives are valuable for nabbing insects before they attack your garden.

Even if the pert little chickadee didn't function as a pest control ally, it would be welcome in your garden. It is the most friendly of garden birds and almost seems to introduce itself as it flies about calling a cheerful "chick-a-dee-dee-dee."

How to attract them. The chickadee frequently is attracted to bits of food in the feeder, especially in the cold winter months when insect eggs are hard to find. Its favorite fare consists of suet, peanut butter, sunflower seeds, bread crumbs, and even broken dog biscuits. Grabbing a seed between its feet, the chickadee will use its sharp beak to hammer the seed open. This trusting mite (only 4½ inches long) may become tame enough to eat seed from your hand or even light on your shoulder as you replenish the feeder.

Besides eating insects and feeder foods, black-capped chickadees seek wild seeds and fruits from plants when available. Seeds and nuts from elms, firs, hemlocks, oaks, pines, and sweet gum trees, and fruit from blueberries, service berries, and Virginia creepers are preferred.

Chickadee relatives. Black-capped chickadees (common residents across the northern states) are honored as the state birds of Maine and Massachusetts. The similar CAROLINA CHICKADEE is found in the Southeast, and the CHESTNUT-BACKED CHICKADEE is found on the West Coast. The MOUNTAIN CHICKADEE, with a black cap and a white line running above each eye, is found in and near western mountains. All can be identified as chickadees by their black crowns, black throats, and white cheeks.

Most chickadees announce their presence with a clear whistled song of two to four notes. The chestnut-backed chickadee, however, lacks its relatives' song quality. It compensates instead with its bright coloring — reddish brown back with reddish brown sides in some regions.

Birds seen year-round. Small flocks of chickadees often forage for their winter food in the company of nuthatches, kinglets, downy woodpeckers, and brown creepers. When the temperature drops at night, the chickadees huddle together for warmth, often seeking the shelter of a deserted bird house. The flocks break up as spring approaches, and pairs of chickadees choose their nesting sites. If you have faithfully fed the bright-eyed chickadees during the winter, they may stay on in a rustic birdhouse, although some will head into the woodlands, searching for a cavity in a decaying stump or an abandoned woodpecker hole.

Incredible insect hunters. Especially during the winter months when many other insect-eating birds have left for sunnier southern areas, the black-capped chickadees will scurry around searching for the eggs of plant lice, spiders, moths, and worms. Their search is so intensive that one bird specialist estimated that a single bird might destroy 138,750 eggs of the cankerworm in just 25 days after the female worm lays them. In measuring this astounding ability to gather food quickly, a professor in Michigan has calculated that chickadees destroy more than eight billion insects each year in his state alone.

Tufted Titmouse

(Member of Chickadee-Titmice family)

■ ALL YEAR

On a bleak, wintry day, you're likely to bring the curious tufted titmouse out of its hiding place in a nearby oak with a "squeaking" sound made by kissing the back of your hand.

Often heard but not seen, the tufted titmouse adds a cheerful note to the garden with its incessant singing of "peeter, peeter." In the spring and early summer this bird never seems to tire of its whistled song, but its human neighbors sometimes grow weary of the repetitive notes.

How to attract them. The sprightly tufted titmouse is a frequent visitor to your winter cafeteria, often picking up its favorite food and returning quickly to a sheltered spot on a tree limb. "Tomtit," as it is popularly called, might reprimand you with harsh chatter unless the feeding tray is filled with its favorite foods like suet, sunflower seeds, bread, doughnuts, raisins, or nut meats.

Besides its regular winter stops at the feeding tray, the titmouse, like its relatives the chickadees, industriously forages for hibernating insects and eggs in tree crevices. During spring and summer, tufted titmice carefully search for caterpillars, wasps, beetles, and other insects. They also eat fruits of elderberry, hackberry, mulberry, wax myrtle, wild strawberry, and seeds and nuts of beech, pine, and oak trees.

Noisy visitors much of the year, tufted titmice are less evident during the breeding season. They may nest in residential areas with dense deciduous trees or will accept birdhouses with entrance holes 1¼ inches in diameter. Perhaps because rustic bird boxes resemble the tree cavities titmice naturally nest in, these woodland birds seem to prefer boxes constructed of wood with the bark still on.

A peaked cap. Dressed in a soft gray feathered coat and a peaked cap, the tufted titmouse is easily distinguished from other small birds. As the "tomtit" hangs its head downward from its arboreal trapeze, its pointed cap often seems on the brink of falling off.

The 6-inch tufted titmouse is the only bird of its size in the eastern states that has a crest. The few other crested birds that may visit your garden are much larger, wearing top knots of red (cardinal), blue (blue jay), and drab brown (cedar waxwing). Other distinguishing marks of the tufted titmouse are its black forehead, white underparts, and reddish-brown flanks.

Year-round residents. The titmouse is seen year-round in the East from Connecticut south to Florida. In recent years, it has been spreading steadily northward. Although nonmigratory, titmice may wander around during winter months in loose flocks with such other resident birds as chickadees, nuthatches, and downy woodpeckers.

Unusual nest lining. In the spring, both sexes of tufted titmice help build a nest of leaves, moss, bark shreds, fur, and hair. The brazen birds have even been known to gather hair for lining their nests by landing on top of a man's head or the back of a dog and pulling out a beakful. Titmice may raise two sets of young during the season. The young often stay with their parents after leaving the nest, until the whole family joins other birds in the fall.

Western relative has crest. The PLAIN TITMOUSE, a western relative of the tufted titmouse, is found in oak, pinon, and juniper woodlands and commonly in tree-shaded suburban areas, city parks, and gardens from Oregon to Wyoming, south to Baja California, and to western Texas. Garbed in dull solid gray, this crested little bird is true to its Latin name of *inornatus*, meaning "unadorned." Like tufted titmice, it nests in tree cavities but also settles in available birdhouses.

Common Bushtit

(Member of Chickadee-Titmice family)

■ ALL YEAR

As though they are playing "follow the leader," bushtits meander through oak trees, garden shrubbery, and street trees in small flocks, looking like tiny fluffs of gray feathers with long tails. Besides their constant movement, bushtits communicate with each other in high-pitched twittering notes. Except when they are breeding or nesting, this sociable bird is always in flocks of 10 to 30 or more. The bushtit seems to be a friendly bird, seldom disturbed by man being nearby.

How to attract them. Bushtits will sample a mixed menu of feeding tray items, especially a mixture of suet, peanut butter, and yellow cornmeal. However, most of a bushtit's diet is insects. Their busy, never-stopping movements in the foliage is in essence an incessant search for insects and spiders. Sometimes bushtits hang upside down from branches to feed.

An artful nest builder. Known for its highly developed skills as an avian architect, the bushtit produces nests that are veritable works of art. At first glance the nest may look like an accumulation of plant debris or perhaps a child's stocking about 8 to 10 inches long. This pendant nest hangs from the outer ends of branches. The camouflage among the foliage is accomplished by the blending of the mosses, lichens, leaves, and spider webs which the bushtit uses to make the nest. The entrance to the nest is near the top on one side of the structure.

Strictly western. Mainly year-round birds of the oak woodlands and chaparral of the Pacific Coast and southwestern states, bushtits are found in large numbers. Higher mountain and desert areas are not suitable habitats for these birds.

White-breasted Nuthatch

(Member of Nuthatch family)

■ ALL YEAR

Not dependent on its tail as a prop (as are woodpeckers and brown creepers), this tree-trunk bird can travel up the trunk of a tree and, with equal ease, turn around and scamper down head first. The stubby, white-breasted nuthatch performs its daring act with only the aid of sharp, curved claws which dig into the tree bark no matter which direction it heads. By working its way down head first, the industrious nuthatch is noted for finding hidden insects that go unnoticed by other birds that are only able to search in an upward direction. The nuthatch sometimes forsakes the trunk to search for insects on the undersides of branches.

How to attract them. White-breasted nuthatches will happily take a break from their insect searching to grab some food from your feeder. Flying in to snatch suet, sunflower seeds, peanut butter, hemp, pumpkin and squash seeds, doughnuts, and nut meats, their visits are normally short. With extreme patience, some people have managed to coax them into feeding from their hands. Whether it is visiting the feeder or scrutinizing tree trunks for food, the nuthatch often pauses to sound its trumpetlike nasal call of "yank-yank."

In addition to the normal feeder food, the gardener can provide a variety of seeds and nuts by planting such trees as beech, fir, maple, oak, pine, and spruce. Berries of the elderberry, mountain ash, and Virginia creeper may also be sampled by the nuthatch.

When spring weather comes, the white-breasts seek nesting sites in the cavities of deciduous trees. To encourage the nuthatches to stay in your garden, a rustic bird box — constructed from a hollowed-out log or bark-covered planks — is essential. Place it under or on a limb of the largest tree in your garden.

A skillful stuntsman. An active, sparrow-sized bird with black cap, white underparts, and stubby tail, the white-breasted nuthatch has been nicknamed the tree mouse,

upside-down bird, or devil-down-head. As the nuthatch makes its way down a tree, it often bends its head backward to a position horizontal with the ground.

Widespread range. The nuthatch hunts insects year-round over much of the United States, enduring the long, cold winters. If you can attract nuthatches to your garden, you'll be rewarded with continuous insect control — destruction of larvae and eggs in the winter and the elimination of ants, beetles, caterpillars, moths, scale insects, and weevils in warmer months.

Relatives like conifers. If you live where conifers are abundant, particularly across the northern United States and in the West as far south as central California and Arizona, you're likely to see the RED-BREASTED NUTHATCH. Besides conifers it also will come to a feeder or nest box. Distinguished by a dark line running through each eye, this bird has the peculiar habit of smearing pitch around the entrance hole of a bird box, just as it does to natural tree cavities in the forest.

The PYGMY NUTHATCH is strictly a bird of the West. Along the central California coast and in mountains from Idaho to the Mexican border, it is commonly seen in towns and gardens with many pines.

Wrentit

(Member of Wrentit family)

ALL YEAR

If you have a lot of patience and time to wait near the wrentit's brushy hiding place, you may catch a glimpse of this elusive bird as it ventures out in the open for a fleeting moment or two. Though they aren't seen very often, the male's loud ringing voice heard throughout the year is a dead giveaway to where they're hiding. The song is a series of dry notes all on the same pitch, culminating in a rapidly run together trill. To many people it sounds like a marble bouncing down the stairs.

How to attract them. Strictly western, the wrentit's range is Oregon, California, and Baja California. They stay in the general vicinity of their birthplace, and are commonly seen among the native scrubby vegetation. But unless you are in its brushy hillside habitat — the chaparral of the Pacific Coast — or living very close to

it, don't expect to see this bird. Although no specific strategy can be used to entice the wrentit into your garden, you might be able to attract it to a birdbath.

Long cocked tail. The wrentit is brown colored and the size of a sparrow. Its long tail, tilted upward, is a major identification feature. Its striking white eye is another characteristic to look for, that is, when you can get close enough to see it. Although it behaves like a wren, it is not related to that family.

Flies short distances. In lowland thickets the wrentit's movements are made up of short hops or flights of a few feet from one shrub to another. It seldom traverses across open space of more than 30 feet. As it moves through the brush, the wrentit jerks its tail quickly from side to side and up and down.

(Continued on next page)

Insects and berries. All year long, wrentits hunt industriously for insects, particularly during the spring and summer when insects are plentiful. Ants and wasps make up a good percentage of this bird's insect intake.

However, it will eat small fruits when a good supply is available, usually fall and winter. Berries of snowberry, elderberry, blackberry, toyon, and other native plants contribute to its list of preferences.

House Wren

(Member of Wren family)

ALL YEAR
SUMMER
WINTER

What do an old tin can, a rural mail box, a discarded straw hat, a clothes pin bag, a drain pipe, and a hole under the eave of a roof have in common? They are a sampling of the odd nooks and crannies often chosen as nesting sites by the house wren when a more respectable cavity isn't available.

How to attract them. Although this wren isn't too particular about housing accommodations, it will readily nest in properly built nest boxes. A simple box with an entrance hole no more than 1¼ inches in diameter will provide perfect accommodations, but many people prefer to buy ready-made little bungalows with peaked roofs.

If you prefer to build your own wren house, make the entrance 1¼ inches high and several inches wide. It will make it easier for the wrens to bring in the dry twigs they use as a base for their bulky nest. Because an entrance this size is big enough for house sparrows to use, be careful not to place the house in the garden until the first wrens arrive in spring. Placement of the house is not important, because, unlike other birds, these little wrens don't seem to care whether their house hangs from a tree limb or is securely nailed to a pole.

Because both young and adult wrens prefer to eat insects almost exclusively through spring and summer, they are readily welcomed in most gardens as valuable pest destroyers. This may help make up for the unfortunate fact that aggressive house wrens sometimes attack the nests of other birds, puncturing the eggs or killing the young.

Known for noise. The modest gray-brown plumage of the house wren is far from distinctive, but you'll remember these birds by their persistent song. Even though they may hide in shrubby undergrowth, they can't resist calling out to proclaim their presence. Out in the open, you'll see them characteristically holding their stubby tails upright.

They span the country. House wrens spend their winters along the southern borders of the United States and in Mexico. Each spring they travel north to nesting grounds across the country, from the Pacific to the Atlantic. In the Southwest (including central and southern California), the wrens are frequent visitors to towns located along streams.

The males arrive ahead of the females and stake out their territories. Once called by an Indian name which meant "big noise for its size," the feisty brown male warns other wrens to keep away with an outpouring of bubbling song. If another wren insists on entering his domain, the male house wren may even aggressively launch an attack.

The male builds many nests. Even before the female appears, the male house wren will busily start building a nest. He generally overdoes it, gathering twigs and scattering them in every available spot. When a female arrives, he courts her with ardent song, showing her his assorted nests. The fussy female selects one and often unceremoniously tosses out his sticks and starts collecting her own. She chatters and scolds as she readies the nest, finally laying six to eight (or as many as twelve) brown-speckled eggs. While she sits on her eggs, her industrious mate may attract a second mate to a nearby nest. If so, he's kept very busy supplying two families with an endless number of spiders, insects, beetles, caterpillars, and grasshoppers.

Larger relatives. The house wren may compete for a spot in your garden with some of its larger relatives. The BEWICK'S WREN (pronounced *Buicks*), has white eye stripes and a white-trimmed fan tail. Its habitat ranges from southwestern British Columbia south to Mexico and in the East from central Pennsylvania to the Gulf states. Like its relatives, the rusty-colored CAROLINA WREN is a fine musician who will visit gardens from New England south to the Gulf states and as far west as Texas. The Carolina is attracted to feeding trays stocked with peanuts, nut meats, and suet. Both Bewick's and Carolina wrens are cavity dwellers who will nest in man-made bird houses, baskets, holes, or tin cans.

The CAÑON WREN is also a backyard bird in canyon or rocky areas of the southwestern states. It enjoys climbing about logs, thickets, and brush piles. Distinctive features of the Cañon are a white throat and upper chest area and a bill that is slightly curved downward and is longer than the bill of the house wren.

In desert gardens, the CACTUS WREN lives in cactus, mesquite, and other desert shrubbery. It is the largest wren in the country, nearly twice the size of the house wren (which is around 4 to 5 inches in length). For food, it forages a good deal on the ground around the bases of desert brush.

Mockingbird

(Member of Mockingbird-Thrasher family)

ALL YEAR

The slender mockingbird is often romantically pictured in a setting symbolic of the Old South — a moonlit night, the rich fragrance of magnolia blossoms, and the mockingbird pouring out its magnificent song. This virtuoso of the bird world also sings its songs around the country from less picturesque perches — backyard fences, power lines, television aerials, chimney tops, and telephone poles.

How to attract them. Most alluring to mockingbirds are gardens with shrubbery to nest in, tree limbs to perch on, and plenty of berries to eat. Mockingbirds often seek food and shelter from the following plants: blackberry, flowering crabapple, grape, honeysuckle, holly, multiflora rose, pyracantha, and red cedar. Other choice fruiting plants that attract these birds are California peppertree, cherry, dogwood, elderberry, manzanita, mulberry, privet, serviceberry, and Virginia creeper.

Even though the mockingbird dines on fruits and berries in all seasons, about half of its diet in warm weather consists of ants, beetles, caterpillars, flies, grasshoppers, lizards, snails, and spiders.

When the berry supply in your garden diminishes, you can keep the mockingbird nearby by stocking your feeder with dried fruit, nutmeats, currants, raisins, suet, and bread crumbs. The pushy mockingbirds may drive smaller birds from the feeding tray. You can also expect these songsters to stop for a splash in your birdbath.

Look for the white patches. In the middle of a song, the gray-colored mockingbird may suddenly leap from his perch, raise his wings high above his body, expose white patches on wings and tail, and float down to earth without dropping a note as his song continues.

Moving northward. Although mockingbirds have been year-round residents from California to Connecticut, they have been gradually extending their eastern range in a northerly direction during the milder seasons, migrating south during the colder times.

Not shy, these birds. Mockers aren't timid about nesting close to your house in vines, bushes, and low trees, usually within 10 feet of the ground. You'll see the male and female at work making a nest of twigs, grass, rootlets, and perhaps a little string. Once finished, the male guards the nest and surrounding territory while the female sits on the four or five brightly colored eggs she has laid. If you try to get close to the nest during this time, the intensely aggressive male mocker may attack. He's well known for successfully fending off all intruders, including roving cats or dogs. Mockers also may fight with other birds of their kind. This fighting instinct often becomes so intense that mockers attack their reflections in hubcaps or big windows, occasionally killing themselves.

Talented tongues. The mockingbird's scientific name is *Mimus polyglottos* (meaning many-tongued mimic) —a name aptly coined as a result of their unusual ability to imitate the calls of other birds. One adept mocker was heard imitating the calls of 32 different birds in 10 minutes. He relished each phrase, rapidly repeating it several times.

The mockingbird's repertoire also contains many original compositions, as well as medleys that are combinations of his repertoire and that of other songbirds.

Relatives of the mockingbird. Although not as accomplished a mimic, the CATBIRD has a pleasing song that is often interwoven with some mimicked tunes.

In summer the catbird may choose quarters in gardens across the United States, except those in the far West and Southwest. It isn't easy to spot this slate-gray bird because it likes to hide in tangled shrubbery. But you can often hear it skulking through bushes, its cat-like "mewing" (the source of its name) readily drawing your attention to its presence.

You can often coax the catbird to your feeder where you can see him eating food left for the mockingbirds.

But his favorite menu will be the fruits and berries ripening on your garden plants.

Having a song similar to the mockingbird are other relatives: the BROWN THRASHER (seen east of the Rockies), the CURVE-BILLED THRASHER (found in desert areas of Arizona and New Mexico), and the CALIFORNIA THRASHER (preferring dense shrubbery in California). Their songs, a succession of mockingbirdlike notes and short phrases, are usually repeated only once or twice.

Robin
(Member of Thrush family)

ALL YEAR
SUMMER
WINTER

Perhaps the best known and among the most abundant of all birds in North America, robins announce spring with their song in gardens around the entire country. In fact, any time you look at a lawn you're likely to see the familiar robin making short runs here and there, stopping to cock its head to the side and then quickly pulling a wiggly earthworm from the ground.

How to attract them. Although robins feed heavily on insects in warm months, they are also fond of fruit. To attract them, plant your garden with berry-bearing shrubs (cotoneaster, mulberry, or pyracantha) and trees (dogwood, mountain ash, Japanese flowering crabapple, or Russian olive). In the East robins coming down from Canada may brave the winter climate even in New England states if plantings of cedar (for shelter) and a supply of winter berries from junipers, hawthorns, sumacs, and bayberries are available.

Preferring a tree crotch, bush, or tangled vine for nesting, robins also will use fence posts, window sills, porch eaves, or open nesting shelves. A pair works together to build a nest of twigs, grass, leaves, and sometimes bits of tissue paper, yarn, and string. The inner cup is made of mud and lined with fine grass. The gardener who provides a shallow cake tin filled with mud will discover robins scooping up beakfuls to carry to their nest.

Look for the red breast. Like the bluebird, the robin is a member of the thrush family — a family of gifted singers. With its blackish head, gray back, and rusty-

red breast, the male robin doesn't look much like the spotted-breast thrushes of the woods, but the speckle-breast young robins give the relationship away. The female looks like the male but is duller in color.

You can use the robin as a guide for judging the size of other birds you see in your garden. It measures about 10 inches from the tip of its yellow bill to the tip of its tail.

They follow a timetable. In early spring robins travel north to breed and raise their families. Like other migrating birds, the robins are on a timetable: they fly north when the days lengthen and the weather gets warm enough to supply them with their favorite foods of insects and berries. The male robin usually arrives at nesting grounds ahead of the female.

After spending the summer in your garden, many robins will fly south to warmer wintering grounds. However, the birds that summered in the far north of Alaska may come only as far south as Washington, Oregon, or central California.

Setting up housekeeping. Finding a perch on the limb of a tree, the robin will stake out a claim to a territory, an area he will defend against birds of his own kind. Beginning almost before daybreak, the robin's melodious notes are actually warnings to any intruder to keep away. The territory, averaging about one-third acre per pair, serves to space the robins so each pair may have an adequate food supply for the critical task of raising a family. Although the robin's song can be a warning to rivals, it also serves to attract a mate.

Robins grow fast, fight hard. The female robin incubates three or four clear blue eggs for about 12 days. When these eggs hatch, the helpless young keep the parents busy in a constant search for snails, earthworms, beetles, caterpillars, grasshoppers, and other small organisms. A hungry young robin in his last day in the nest may eat the equivalent of 14 feet of earthworms. Young robins grow so rapidly from the constant feeding by their parents that they have reached adult size by the time they leave the nest. Although they have left the nest, the young fledglings are taken care of for a time by the male while the female prepares her nest for another brood of young.

In his established territory, the robin is ready to grapple with any rival. In his eagerness to defend, this bird often mistakes his own reflection in a window or hubcap for an intruder and can be seen pecking vigorously at or buffeting himself against his own image. Off and on, he may keep this up for several days. If you see this happening, you can protect the robin from possible injury by screening the car window or by moving the car.

ALL YEAR
SUMMER
WINTER

Eastern Bluebird
(Member of Thrush family)

The handsome bluebird has always been a favorite with many bird watchers and has occasioned many a line of prose or verse from writers taken with its beauty. Both John Burroughs and Henry Thoreau described the bluebird as a bird of heaven and earth because of its sky-blue back and earthen-red breast. Naturally a cavity nester, the bluebird has always favored the rotted hollows of aging apple trees, but in the 20th century these sites have become a rarity. As a result, the population of this popular bird of happiness has sharply declined.

How to attract them. In response to the bluebirds' housing shortage, many residents of communities across the country have set out boxes on fence posts along rural roads. If you live in an area that is still fairly rural, you might want to join the campaign by putting up boxes in your garden. Because they are territorial birds like their cousins, the robins, only one couple of bluebirds is likely to set up housekeeping in a garden. Raising two or three broods in a season, the birds may alternately nest in more than one house.

Because intruding starlings and house sparrows often claim squatter's rights to a bluebird box, take these two precautions to help the bluebirds compete more successfully for a home: (1) the entrance hole to the box should be no larger than 1½ inches to prevent the larger starlings from entering, and (2) because house sparrows generally prefer higher sites, place the box only 5 feet above the ground.

In addition to the bird box, your garden should also offer a shallow birdbath and plants that provide winter fruits and berries. Such shrubs as blackberry, blueberry, bayberry, wild cherry, cotoneaster, Virginia creeper, dogwood, holly, mulberry, pyracantha, sumac, and viburnum should be the most tempting. Enhancing all these attractants is a garden with a fertile lawn harboring a sumptuous feast of insects of many varieties — the main course for the bluebird's warm weather dining.

Bluebirds East and West. The eastern bluebird is seen east of the Rockies and ranges from Canada to the Gulf states. It migrates to southern parts for the winter and often heads north before spring begins. The WESTERN BLUEBIRD is adorned in the same handsome colors as its eastern counterpart, but its back has an extra patch of rusty-red and its throat is blue. This western bird also has the bad posture characteristic of eastern bluebirds: when perching, their shoulders appear hunched. Even though the western bluebird will seek shelter in bird boxes, it often spends summers in the mountains, descending to lower valleys for the winter.

The MOUNTAIN BLUEBIRD is even shyer than its relatives. Clad in a turquoise-blue suit (it has no red breast), this state bird of Idaho and Nevada breeds in tree cavities and boxes at high elevations. From its home in the upper reaches, it only ventures into lower parts when cold weather comes.

COPING WITH UNWANTED BIRD GUESTS

A favorite berry bush, a rustic birdhouse, selected bird seed placed in the feeder — all these enticements will help to bring birds into your garden. But some birds don't require any coaxing to come around; in fact, they will probably come without an invitation. The bad manners of these gate crashers may even place them at the top of your "least wanted" bird list.

Pigeons, grackles, blackbirds, jays, and cowbirds often fall into this category. But, in sheer numbers, house sparrows and starlings (two highly adaptable European immigrants) are likely to be the most disruptive birds in your garden. Below are brief descriptions (if you're not already acquainted) of these scalawags of the bird world.

HOUSE SPARROWS, although they resemble many of our native sparrows, were imported from England after 1850 and introduced in several places around the country. Also called English sparrows, these birds now span the continent and are perhaps the most commonly known small birds.

In spring the cocky little male (6 inches long) sports a black bib and bill, white cheeks, and a chestnut nape. Without the stark black throat, females and young resemble countless other sparrows with their dull brown coloring on top and whitish coloring below.

Prolific breeders, house sparrows often raise several families from early spring until fall, and sometimes throughout the winter. They build their bulky, structureless nests in any sort of cavity — a nook under rafters, a tree cavity, or a birdhouse. A fearless bully, the house sparrow will even evict birds from their nests, destroying eggs or young.

STARLINGS are also commonly seen. The millions found in all parts of the United States descend from a mere 100 birds introduced into New York's Central Park around 1890 (supposedly by individuals who hoped to bring all the birds Shakespeare mentioned in his works into this country).

The 8-inch-long starling looks like a blackbird, but its tail is much shorter. The adult's plumage varies by season. In the fall, its black feathers are speckled with tiny "stars" and its bill is dusky. In the spring, the bill turns bright yellow and its shiny black coat is glossed with iridescent purple and green. Young starlings are a dull gray-brown color.

Like the house sparrow, starlings breed rapidly, stuffing nests of twigs into available hollows and producing two or even three broods each year. In the fall, flocks of thousands join together, flying in formation with amazing precision and roosting communally throughout the winter over much of the country.

Both usurp nesting sites. Abundant in numbers, starlings and house sparrows challenge other nesting birds for available nesting cavities.

If starlings or house sparrows frequent your garden, the struggle to keep them away may sometimes seem hopeless. But experienced bird attracters have found some success by adhering to these points:

(1) Keep the opening to your birdhouse 1½ inches or smaller in diameter. This will keep the chunky starling out but not the smaller house sparrow.

(2) Prevent martin houses from being taken over by these intruders (who often nest early in the spring) by not putting up the houses (or blocking the entrance) until the first martins arrive.

(3) Don't put perches under birdhouse openings. Nesting native birds can do without them, and starlings and house sparrows welcome a perch to sit on and bother the birds inside.

(4) If you're intent on driving them away, make repeated attempts to eliminate or remove their nests.

Both monopolize feeding stations. House sparrows and starlings may bully other birds at a feeder, particularly if it's an open tray. Here are a few tricks to help keep these rascals away:

(1) To attract smaller birds like the chickadees, put out food in a feeder that swings from a tree branch (this tends to frighten larger birds). A glassed-in window feeder with a small entrance hole also gives little birds an undisturbed chance to feed. But be patient; it's usually difficult to get birds started on this type of a feeder.

(2) Because they are ground feeders, you can sometimes lure house sparrows and starlings away from your main feeders by scattering grain and stale bread crumbs on a nearby patch of ground.

(3) Don't put perches on all your suet logs or the other birds won't even get a taste.

They're a mixed blessing. The only absolute way to rid your garden of pesty birds is to trap them. But that's an extreme step. Even starlings and house sparrows aren't all bad. Starlings help protect your lawn by feeding on beetle grubs and other damaging insects.

In general, house sparrows are less welcome than starlings, but their ingenious antics can be entertaining, particularly on a bleak winter day when most birds are further south. You'll appreciate their "intelligence" when you put out a new feeder and they are the first to find it. Their presence alerts shyer species to your offerings, even though they will have to wait until the hungry sparrows relinquish their places at the feeder.

Ruby-crowned Kinglet

(Member of Kinglet family)

ALL YEAR
SUMMER
WINTER

Flitting about your garden in winter, the animated ruby-crowned kinglet probably will be inspecting the ends of tree branches for the eggs and larvae of insects. This ability to dig out insects from areas that larger birds can't reach makes the kinglets valuable garden allies.

How to attract them. In addition to foraging for insects in garden trees, the industrious kinglets will scout feeding trays for suet, peanuts, and cracked nuts.

Although they usually nest in dense evergreen forests, kinglets may also breed in northern gardens containing conifers like fir or spruce.

Plain-colored females. Male kinglets can often be distinguished from females by the brightly colored crowns they wear, but the male is likely to keep his fiery red patch concealed except when excited. The olive-colored female lacks this red adornment. A white eye ring, which gives the impression of staring, is an easier identification mark.

Head north in spring. The tiny kinglets winter across the country, from the Pacific and southwestern states into Mexico and from Kentucky and Maryland south to the Gulf states. When nesting time arrives, they seek the higher elevations of western mountains and coniferous forests of the northern states and Canada.

Beautiful breeding song. While its winter voice is just short bursts of chatter, you may be lucky enough to hear a bit of the ruby-crown's magnificent breeding song before it heads for northern wilds. It's a beautiful, warbling composition, astonishingly strong for a bird so small.

Golden-crowned relatives. The kinglet's musical talent is not shared with the closely related GOLDEN-CROWNED KINGLET, but they're alike in many other habits. The golden-crowns also visit winter gardens across the United States (including those in the Northeast), but they return each spring to conifers in the North or in western mountains and coastal canyons.

They're easily recognized as kinglets by the nervous twitching of their wings. If you look closely, you'll see the characteristic crowns of both sexes — gold bordered with touches of black and white. An added stripe of bright orange runs down the center of the male's crown.

Cedar Waxwing

(Member of Waxwing family)

ALL YEAR
SUMMER
WINTER

Flying evenly in close ranks above the tree tops, a squad of 10 to 20 cedar waxwings will arrive in your area. Suddenly they'll wheel around and descend into a garden for a meal of mulberries or any available ripe fruit. The handsome cedar waxwings are popularly nicknamed "cedar" or "cherry" birds because of their reputation for devouring fruit, particularly from cherry and cedar trees.

(Continued on next page)

How to attract them. If your garden has choice fruit and berry plants and provides a birdbath or pool for drinking and bathing, you're likely to be visited by these gentle-mannered birds.

A shrubby berry-bearing border around your yard is a likely way to attract their attention. Any of these plants are good choices: apple, cotoneaster, crabapple, dogwood, elderberry, elaeagnus, mountain ash, mulberry, privet, pyracantha, shadbush, and of course, cherry and cedar.

In spring and summer, waxwings also feed on insects, often catching them in the air in flycatcher fashion. In addition to destroying thousands of cankerworms, they eat ants, beetles, crickets, and flies.

A pair of waxwings will build their nest of twigs and grass in orchards or in isolated trees and bushes. Potential nesting sites in garden trees include apple, arborvitae (eastern), cedar, maple, and Russian olive.

When winter berries become scarce in northern regions, pieces of raw apple and other cut-up fruit and raisins can be offered as feeder food.

Aristocratic bearing. The beautiful sleek-bodied cedar waxwing can easily be recognized by its silky, fawn-brown plumage and black-masked crested head. It often perches in an erect, aristocratic position, with its short, yellow-tipped tail pointed downward. The waxwing gets its name from the tiny waxy red "droplets" on the tips of its wing feathers.

No strict schedule. A fondness for fruit seems to keep waxwings wandering about the United States during much of the year, but they follow no strict schedule in their travels. They can be seen in various areas in one year but be completely missing other years. After wintering as far south as Panama, they journey north to breed across the northern parts of this country, even into Canada. They are late nesters (June to September), probably waiting for the fruit to ripen so they can feed it to their young.

He hops, she hops. Traveling in winter flocks, waxwings have time to get acquainted with one another, before pairing off in the spring. Because both sexes look alike, the songless male seems to perform a courtship dance in order to identify himself. He may start by carrying a berry to another bird, approaching with a sideways hop. In turn, a responsive female may take the food with the same hopping gesture. The pair may repeat the dance, usually ending it when the female eats the food.

Although cedar waxwings guard their nesting territories. they still continue to gather food with waxwing neighbors. The birds eat voraciously but are extremely sociable while doing so. Sometimes, perched together on a branch, several waxwings will pass some tidbit (a ripe berry or a worm) from bill to bill all along the row and back again, but no bird seems impolite enough to actually eat it. You might expect to hear singing or loud chatter from such a gathering, but the waxwing flock sits together quietly, occasionally offering only soft and high-pitched whistling "zeees."

Another waxwing. The only other North American member of the waxwing family, the BOHEMIAN WAXWING, is found mainly in the northwestern United States. Closely resembling the cedar waxwing in both habits and appearance, the bohemian waxwing is slightly larger and has yellow and white on its wings as well as the characteristic red "droplets." Its appearance pattern is far more erratic than that of the cedar waxwing.

Yellow Warbler

(Member of Wood Warbler family)

SUMMER

Exquisitely dressed in plumage of bright colors, dainty little wood warblers flit from tree to tree, using slender, pointed bills to pick out insects hidden in arboreal nooks and crannies. Unfortunately, as the name implies, wood warblers generally keep to the wild woods, visiting gardens only during migration flights. But if you live in a moist climate or near a stream lined with deciduous trees, one member of the wood warbler family — the familiar yellow warbler — won't mind settling in your garden for the entire summer. Its sunshine-yellow coloring and its fondness for insects make this bird a welcome guest.

How to attract them. Because it seeks the tropics during the winter, the yellow warbler can only be attracted to your garden during the warm months. This relatively tame little bird often chooses a garden for nesting if it has low trees, hedges, or ornamental shrubs. It's even friendly enough to build its felted nest in a privet bush next to your porch or in a honeysuckle vine outside the back door. Other nesting sites, generally within 10 feet of the ground, may be found in barberries, currants, grape vines, wild roses, viburnum, and trees such as alder or elder. Outside the garden, it especially loves willow trees on the banks of streams and elms lining streets or boulevards.

If your garden has ample foliage plants, it will provide yellow warblers with the insects they require. Warblers may also sample juicy fruits of mulberries or raspberries. A birdbath is often inviting enough for a delicate warbler splash.

Mistaken for wild canary. At a glance, this warbler appears all yellow, but the male's breast is actually streaked with rusty-brown, and its back carries tones of olive. Across the warbler's wide range, the intensity of its color varies from brighter orange to pale yellow. The feathers of females and young have less brilliant colors of olive and pale yellow, but the birds are distinguished as yellow warblers by yellow spots on their tails.

The yellow warbler is frequently mistaken for another common garden bird, the American goldfinch. Both wear yellow, but the goldfinch has a black crown, black wings and tail, and a short conical beak.

Early departure south. After raising their families across the United States and Canada, yellow warblers make a surprisingly early departure for tropical wintering grounds. They leave their nests almost as soon as the young are able to take care of themselves.

Plagued by the cowbird. Noted for never building nests of their own, cowbirds lay their eggs in the nests of other species. Yellow warblers are often victims of this practice. Some warblers tolerate the strange new eggs and raise the cowbird nestlings as their own; others attempt to outwit the parasitic bird by building a new nest floor over the cowbird eggs. Some birds will add as many as five new floors. The little warblers occasionally cover up their own eggs in their haste to get the job done.

Other warblers stick out the winter. Two familiar wood warblers hardy enough to remain in gardens for the winter are subspecies of the YELLOW-RUMPED WARBLER species. MYRTLE WARBLER, named for its alleged fondness for wax myrtle berries, resides mainly in the eastern United States. In the West it winters from northwest Oregon to southern California and Arizona. Living strictly in the West is the AUDUBON'S WARBLER. As it migrates north, you'll recognize the myrtle by its coat of black, gray and white and four distinct patches of bright yellow on the rump, crown, and sides. The Audubon's warbler has an additional yellow patch on the throat, as well as large white wing patches. Females are duller colored in both cases.

Yellow-rumped warblers breed in coniferous forests in the far North but often like to winter in southern states or along eastern and western coastal areas. They seek winter berries of red cedar or juniper and happily eat suet placed in feeding trays. Both wear duller brown plumage in the colder months, turning to their much brighter characteristic plumage in breeding season.

Northern Oriole

(Member of Oriole-Blackbird family)

SUMMER

Brilliant flashes of black and orange in the tall trees may be a signal that an oriole is in your garden. If it's about the size of a blackbird, chances are it's the northern oriole — a name given to both the Baltimore oriole of the East and the Bullock oriole of the West.

How to attract them. Stock your feeder with a variety of nutmeats and berries (cherry, fig, elderberry, mulberry, blackberry, and serviceberry). They will also eat beef suet, sugar syrup, apple, and orange halves. If

you have a birdbath, chances are the orioles may use it. Another suggestion is to hang up bits of string and darning thread. They may be enticed to collect them for building nests.

A pendant nest. Northern orioles nest in a wide choice of trees, generally high up. City street and boulevard trees, fruit trees, and trees of the open countryside are the main arenas for their courtship antics and nesting activities. The eager males, who arrive a few days earlier than the more modest-looking females, begin flamboyant displays of their black, orange, and white colors. Raising up its wings, spreading out its tail, bowing its head, and flashing its bright hues, the male does its best to attract the female.

Once paired off, it is the female who skillfully weaves the nest. For example, in a tall maple or elm, the female hangs long strands of fibers and grasses over the twigs near the ends of the branches, fastens the strands to make a hanging framework, and finally weaves them together. The nest hangs from the branch like a long open bag or purse.

Orioles that nest in cities and towns use materials collected from the immediate environment —

string, yarn, and horsehair. These bits of material are intricately interwoven to form a smooth, finished nest. If the woven fabrics are sturdy enough, the birds may return to re-use or reinforce the nest the following year. Nevertheless, the birds seem to come back to the same nesting site annually.

Insect hunting in foliage. Orioles search vigorously for insects among the upper foliage of trees. Chief insect prey consist of soft-bodied caterpillars. Ants, bugs, beetles, wasps, grasshoppers, and spiders are other targets. Keep a sharp eye out for these bright-colored birds among the tops of tall trees in the spring and summer months as the orioles bobble and swing from the outer branches.

Cardinal

(Member of Finch-Sparrow-Grosbeak family)

ALL YEAR

Christmas card scenes often show a crested red bird on an evergreen bough against a snowy backdrop. The well known cardinal is just as striking when seen against the spring blossoms of a dogwood. From this tree perch, the male's bright plumage is complemented by the loud clear whistle of his vigorous song. His less flamboyant mate, unlike most females of the bird world, often responds with a softer song that some listeners find even more pleasing than the male's. The birds sometimes sing in unison, swaying their bodies from side to side.

How to attract them. You can host a handsome cardinal family if your garden provides the dense shrubbery they like. For nesting, cardinals seek hedgerows, tangled vines, bushy borders, small trees, or protected thickets. They stay away from open spaces or tree tops (except to take a singing break). Plantings of blackberry, cherry, greenbriar, grape, honeysuckle, multiflora rose, and viburnums will provide nesting sites and food for these birds. The cardinal also feeds on fruit from dogwood, elaeagnus, mulberry, hackberry, raspberry, and sumac.

With its large, conical beak, the cardinal (sometimes called cardinal grosbeak) is well equipped to crack seeds. It looks for weed seeds and grains in the wild but doesn't need much coaxing to stay in your garden

for sunflower seeds at a swinging or platform feeder. These red birds like just about everything provided at a feeder, especially bread, raisins, scratch feed, cracked corn, nutmeats, and squash seeds. Often first at the feeder each morning, a cardinal dominates the scene and, in breeding season, becomes intolerant of fellow cardinals. Although primarily seed eaters, cardinals catch insects, particularly when feeding their young.

Red birds with black masks. Both male and female cardinals wear masks of black around thick coral beaks, but only the male displays brilliant scarlet feathers. The female is more somberly dressed in olive-green with dull red wings and tail. The young resemble their mother. A distinctive trait of all cardinals is their pointed crest.

Spreading northward. Once known exclusively as a bird of the South, the cardinal is one of many birds gradually extending their ranges northward. The cardinal now lives as far north as the Canadian border. Because it's virtually nonmigratory, the bird depends on winter feeding stations for food rations.

Cardinals are widespread east of the Plains states, but they are also found in the southwestern states — generally from central Arizona to northern Texas and south to British Honduras.

Males fight. Cardinals fly in pairs throughout the year, but in winter they sometimes socialize with neighboring cardinals. However, when spring comes, they stick to their chosen territory. Unmated male cardinals often have violent contests while searching for a mate. Once paired off, the female chooses a site in protected shrubbery and builds a loose nest of twigs.

Particularly in the South, a pair of cardinals may raise as many as three families between March and July. The female alone incubates the eggs, but when the newly hatched young are hungry, the male brings them meals of beetles, caterpillars, and scale insects.

Once fashionable cage birds. Although they now enjoy complete freedom under the law, cardinals once suffered the fate of living as cage birds. After living in captivity for a time, a cardinal often faded in color and its song became monotonous.

Black-headed Grosbeak

(Member of Finch-Sparrow-Grosbeak family)

SUMMER

Whatever bird family they belong to, brightly colored male birds generally leave nesting tasks to their mates, perhaps because their presence draws too much attention. But the black-headed grosbeak and his eastern cousin, the ROSE-BREASTED GROSBEAK, are exceptions. Not only does the brilliantly colored male take his turn sitting on the eggs but he often sings loudly while doing so.

How to attract them. Grosbeaks frequent deciduous or evergreen woodlands but will spend their summers in gardens rich in shade trees and low shrubbery. Both the western and eastern species build flimsy nests in shrubs or trees (apples, maples, or elms) at heights 6 to 12 feet from the ground. The nests are so loosely constructed that you can stand below and count the number of eggs (usually three or four).

As their name implies, grosbeaks have large bills that are useful for cracking seeds. But these birds also eat noxious insects in summer — beetles, scale insects, and caterpillars. The rose-breasted grosbeak has gained itself the name of "potato-bug bird" because of its unusual fondness for that insect. These insect-eating habits help some gardeners to overlook the grosbeaks' occasional fondness for planted peas or cultivated fruit. You can satisfy their taste for fruit by planting blackberries, wild cherries, dogwoods, hawthorns, serviceberries, and viburnums.

Although grosbeaks commonly seek the hanging seeds of such trees as maples, you can attract them to feeders stocked with sunflower seeds. Their large beaks adeptly crack the seeds open — in fact, your grosbeak visitors are so good at hulling and eating sunflower seeds that you might have to stretch your seed budget a bit.

Brighter males, duller females. Resembling an overgrown sparrow, the female grosbeak is plain in color. The male is regally attired with a black head contrasting nicely with orange underparts and black and white wings. The male rose-breast is nearly all black and white except for a large triangle of red on his breast.

Summer birds only. Both grosbeaks breed in the United States after wintering farther south. The black-head spends the colder months mainly in Mexico, then migrates into the western parts of the United States and Canada. In the eastern stretches of its range, along the Rocky Mountains, the black-head may hybridize with the rose-breasted grosbeak. The rose-breast's breeding area extends east of the Rockies from Kansas to the Atlantic and from Georgia north to Canada.

Two more grosbeaks. Another handsome grosbeak may visit your garden, wearing dull yellow on its body and black on its tail, wings, and crown. The bird's name, EVENING GROSBEAK, is misleading because it does not keep itself hidden during the day. This striking bird was once regarded as a rare bird of the western coniferous forests, but during the last century it has moved east. The evening grosbeak now nests in the New England states and winters irregularly as far south as Kentucky and Missouri. Wintering flocks across the country have acquired a ravenous appetite for sunflower seeds and other nut meats. They also devour naturally available supplies of fruits and seeds.

Approaching the size of a robin, the PINE GROSBEAK is the largest of the grosbeaks. Its coloring is mostly rose-red, but its wings are black with two prominent white bars. It visits gardens in the winter but prefers high coniferous forests.

House Finch

(Member of Finch-Sparrow-Grosbeak family)

ALL YEAR
WINTER

The house finch brings a flash of red to the garden. Wearing bright scarlet on his head, breast, and rump, the male house finch should be a conspicuous face at your feeder. But his mate is likely to arrive unnoticed. With her streaked, drab brown plumage, she looks like many other sparrow relatives.

How to attract them. As their name implies, house finches often stick close to human habitation, where offerings of food and shelter help to make life a little easier. Almost any sheltered spot in a western garden is a suitable site for the messy nest built by the female. She's fond of choosing a site in vines or hedges around a porch, on a nearby shelf, in a birdhouse (2-inch entrance), or in any other available cranny. While the female nests, the male brightens the garden with his song.

A pair of house finches may raise two or even three sets of young during the nesting season. To feed them, the parents search for some insects but mainly concentrate on soft fruits and berries. It's this taste for fruit (earlier in the season it's buds and blossoms) that has given the house finch a nasty reputation among commercial fruit growers. You'll probably be willing to share a good portion of the cultivated fruit in your garden, but if not, plant berry-bearing wild shrubs to help lure the birds away. Favorite plantings include such shrubs and vines as honeysuckle, lemonade berry, lilac, red flowering currant, elderberry, and dwarf snowberry, and such seed-bearing trees as the sycamore and willow.

Despite complaints against house finches' fruit eating habits, about seven-eighths of their diet is seeds, not fruit. Although they naturally eat weed seeds, you can provide a garden seed source with annuals — marigolds, nasturtiums, or sunflowers.

Your feeding tray will provide a gathering place for the sociable finches. They'll eat almost anything, but seem to prefer sunflower seeds, wild bird seed mixture, hemp and millet, bread, and cut-up fruit.

Abundant in West. The adaptive house finches are abundant throughout western states, making themselves at home in gardens, as well as in open woodlands, scrubby growth, and even in the desert.

Slowly but surely, house finches have even invaded the East. Apparently, in 1940, house finches shipped from the West were illegally sold in New York pet shops as "Hollywood finches." When authorities stopped the sales, dealers probably released the birds. The house finches gained a foothold around New York City and soon spread to Connecticut, southern New Jersey, and beyond. The house finch was also introduced to Hawaii earlier in this century.

"Purple" relatives. In the East and far West, house finches may get a little winter competition when their relatives, the PURPLE FINCHES, arrive from forest breeding grounds. The "purple" in their name is misleading because the male's plumage is washed with rose-red, but his flanks lack the brown streaks of the male house finch. The female is inconspicuously adorned in streaks of brown and white and has a broad, whitish line behind her eyes.

The purple finch is widespread, breeding in the northern forests of the United States and parts of Canada and wintering over most of the country except for the Rocky Mountains and Plains states. Purple finches forage winter feeders for seeds, especially sunflower seeds. Favorite food plants include white ash, American elm, dogwood, honeysuckle, privet, sweetgum, sycamore, and tulip trees.

Another "purple" relative is the CASSIN'S FINCH, a visitor to gardens in the Rocky Mountains and Great Basin areas in the winter. It is very similar to the purple finch in most respects.

American Goldfinch

(Member of Finch-Sparrow-Grosbeak family)

ALL YEAR
SUMMER
WINTER

In the spring when most birds pair off and busily begin constructing their nests, the carefree little goldfinches continue to socialize in small bands. They bounce through the air as if they were riding a roller coaster, calling out cheerful strains of "per-chic-oree."

How to attract them. The American goldfinch dwells in open country, weedy fields, and suburban gardens. It nests in small trees or woody shrubs like dogwood and hawthorn, as well as larger birches, elms, and maples.

Goldfinches may choose to nest in your garden if a bountiful supply of seeds is available. These birds love eating seeds in flower heads, particularly sunflowers and dandelions. Weedy patches near fence corners can provide an automatic seed supply for goldfinches (weedy fields nearby also draw these birds). But the more immaculate gardener could plant attractive annuals like cosmos, bachelor's button, zinnia, or coreopsis.

Flocks of goldfinches readily come to a feeder for wild bird seed mixture, millet, and sunflower seeds.

Males change costume in winter. True to its name, the goldfinch is noted for its yellow color. However, in the winter it's hard for the bird novice to recognize the goldfinch because the male changes his bright yellow

and black summer plumage for the duller, faded olive that the inconspicuous female wears year-round.

The ubiquitous goldfinch. American goldfinches are permanent residents over much of the United States, although a general southern shift occurs for the winter. Attesting to its popularity across the entire country, the American goldfinch is the state bird of Washington, Ohio, and New Jersey.

Efficient nest builder. The goldfinch doesn't settle down to raising a family until midsummer when its chosen fare of seeds are ripe enough to feed their hungry young. This is about the time when the wild thistle provides both seeds and down for lining the bird's compact nest. The felted nest, built almost entirely by the female, is so tightly woven that it will hold rainwater for several hours.

A green-backed cousin. The male LESSER GOLDFINCH is bright yellow below with a black cap, dark greenish back, and white wing patches. In contrast, the American goldfinch flashes a white rump. Less widely distributed than the American goldfinch, the lesser goldfinch nests earlier than the American goldfinch.

Rufous-sided Towhee

(Member of Finch-Sparrow-Grosbeak family)

ALL YEAR
SUMMER
WINTER

The rufous-sided towhee persistently seeks shelter in brushy undergrowth, especially those spots with plenty of dead leaves and twigs to rummage around in. Al-

though towhees like to be out of sight, they don't mind being heard. A pair of these birds will noisily rustle around in leaf litter, vigorously poking about for insects, fallen seeds, and berries. In addition to rustling sounds, you'll probably hear their calls of "towhee" or "che-wink" (another popular name of the bird).

How to attract them. If your garden is too well-manicured, this ground bird won't come around. Instead, it will search for a garden that has plenty of shrubbery around the edges and, perhaps, a tangled thicket.

Towhees feed on insects found close to the ground and are attracted to plants providing both cover and food. Favorite bushes include blackberry, blueberry, elaeagnus, holly, raspberry, and serviceberry. They also like ground covers (such as wild strawberry) that provide easily accessible fruit and trees (such as pine and oak) that drop seeds.

Other food — crumbs, seeds, grains, nutmeats — regularly scattered on the ground close to the shrubbery will provide further encouragement for towhees to nest in your garden. After feeding, the rufous-sided towhee is likely to cool off in a backyard birdbath.

A touch of white. White feathers on its long tail and rounded wings are familiar marks on the towhee. Not much of an aviator, only occasionally does this ground bird fly to the tops of trees to sing. Most of its time is spent rummaging around on the ground and in low bushes.

With black head and back, the male is darker than the female, but both are marked as towhees by the rufous (reddish-brown) sides and white middle belly.

Towhee variety. Ranging across the country, as many as 15 different types (subspecies) of towhees are recognized. White spots dot the backs and shoulders of western types, often called spotted towhees. Northeastern towhees are red-eyed, but in the Southeast they may be white-eyed.

Camouflaged female. After a courtship period (including a chase through the thicket), the female builds a carefully concealed nest on or near the ground. Her brown head and back add to the camouflage. If you come too close to the nest, she may scurry away, even feigning injury to distract attention from the eggs.

Her aggressive mate zealously guards their territory, often trying to fight his reflection in a window.

Brown Towhee

(Member of Finch-Sparrow-Grosbeak family)

ALL YEAR

Naturally a bird of the brushlands, the brown towhee readily accepts the dense shrubbery of gardens and parks as a substitute for its native bushy cover. One of the commonest birds lurking in California gardens, the brown towhee appears so plain in its dull brown garb that it might pass by unnoticed except for its persistent metallic "chink" call.

How to attract them. In your garden, an open lawn offers a good source of insects for the towhee, and an ornamental shrubbery border provides nesting sites for this year-round resident. In addition to exotic plants such as the glossy privet and laurustinus, you might provide the following native chaparral plants: silktassel, toyon, cascara sagrada, manzanita, mahonia, sugar bush, or wild lilac. Pines and native oaks are other brushland favorites suitable for garden planting.

In addition to fruit-bearing shrubs (and perhaps a tangled corner of blackberry or raspberry), you can scatter commercial bird seed mixture or bread crumbs on the lawn. The white-crowned sparrows and other smaller ground feeders will be attracted to the food, but the brown towhee will dominate the scene, often squabbling over a few seeds. A feeding tray stocked with crumbs, seeds, and scraps will also attract the towhee.

Strong legs. Never straying too far, this weak-winged bird depends on its strong legs for locomotion. More like an overgrown sparrow than a towhee, the brown towhee likes to forage for food in the open but wants to be close enough to cover to be able to take advantage of it if necessary.

Only in the West. The brown towhee resides west of the Sierras from Oregon in the north to Baja California in the south. The grayer forms in Arizona, New Mexico, Colorado, and Texas are sometimes called CAÑON TOWHEES.

Aggressive male. During the breeding season, the male brown towhee becomes particularly difficult to get along with, boldly berating other birds of its kind who unwisely trespass on his territory. Often the towhee will become so excited that he vigorously fights his own reflection in a window or hubcap for days on end.

Slight garden damage. Gardeners will welcome the insect and weed seed eating habits of the brown towhee, but it's hard to accept its fondness for sprouted seeds in a carefully tilled garden. You can often keep its sharp eye away from seedlings by scattering seeds elsewhere. But just to make sure the towhee stays away, protect young plants with fine wire netting.

Dark-eyed Junco

(Member of Finch-Sparrow-Grosbeak family)

ALL YEAR
SUMMER
WINTER

Hungrily eating the wild bird seed offered at your feeding tray, chickadees and nuthatches often kick part of their food to the ground. Dark-eyed juncos (formerly the Oregon juncos, slate-colored juncos, and white-winged juncos were considered as separate species) like this because they prefer rummaging for food from the ground. You can give the dark-eyed juncos and other sparrows some assistance in feeding by regularly sprinkling seed on the ground below the feeder.

How to attract them. Although they naturally seek seeds from weeds growing by roadsides and brushy open spaces, juncos welcome a treat of scattered bread crumbs, walnut meats, sunflower seeds, and assorted grain. Suet and peanut butter (mixed with cornmeal so the birds don't choke) will help warm them up, especially on cold winter days. And a well landscaped garden with plenty of shrubbery offers a retreat from the wind.

White on tail. These nervous little birds venture out into open areas only if they can fly to cover at the slightest sign of danger (such as a prowling cat). When a small flock of juncos flies into the bushes, the last thing you'll see is a flash of white on their outer tail feathers. The birds' coloration varies among subspe-

cies. Most Oregon juncos wear a black hood that contrasts with a rusty back.

Lowlands in winter. Retreating from the cold of the mountains where they summer, Oregon juncos spend their winters foraging for seeds in the Western lowlands as far south as Mexico. Occasionally, this junco will wander to feeders in eastern states.

Eastern snowbirds. It's more common to see the slate-colored juncos venturing into eastern gardens. Their gray back blends into a hood of the same coloring, distinguishing them from their other relatives—the white-winged junco (white wing bars with a gray back) and the gray-headed junco (ashy gray sides and wings, but rufous-colored back).

Although the winter range of slate-colored juncos extends across the country, they are most abundant in eastern states and almost absent in the Pacific states. Called "snowbirds" in the Northeast, their arrival from breeding grounds in coniferous forests generally signals the onset of winter. Slate-colored juncos can brave a snow storm if you scatter small grain seeds or plant seed-bearing annuals, such as the tall amaranths, which hold their seeds high above the snow.

Chipping Sparrow

(Member of Finch-Sparrow-Grosbeak family)

ALL YEAR
SUMMER
WINTER

Although your ears may pick up what sounds like a sewing machine or an electric sharpener, actually the noise could be the dry, monotonous trill of the chipping sparrow. This trusting, friendly little sparrow is

donned with a reddish cap and a white line over each eye. Watch for it in your garden or on your lawn looking for food. Parks, orchards, and farmyards are other places it searches for food.

(Continued on next page)

How to attract them. Chipping sparrows are highly adaptable to a broad slate of habitats. Aside from the open spaces they need and find in lawn areas, yards, and the like, they visit gardens with lots of foliage to establish nesting sites. Ornamental shrubs, clinging vines, and trees in the garden area attract this sparrow. Rose thickets seem to be a big favorite. If you are host to the "chip bird," try feeding it in person. In some cases it has become so tame, it has taken food right from a person's hand.

Hairlined nest. Usually this bird builds its nest about 5 feet from the ground in selected dense vegetation. If you get a chance to peek at its architecture, you'll probably find the nest lined with black horsehair or a material that closely resembles it. Because the chipping sparrow characteristically uses hair in this fashion, it is often dubbed the hair-bird. Grasses and fine roots are also used to construct the fragile cup-shaped nest. Only three or four days are needed to make the nest from start to finish.

Foster parents of cowbirds. Because they don't make a nest of their own, female cowbirds often lay an egg in the chipping sparrow's nest. Their deposited eggs are hatched and their young are cared for by the chipping sparrows who apparently take this in stride, raising the nestlings until they can care for themselves.

Weed seeds and insects. In summer, insects (especially soft-bodied caterpillars) make up the bulk of the chipping sparrow's diet. Gypsy moths, beet worms, and grasshoppers are other favored morsels. Its staple diet during other seasons consists of weed seeds. The seeds of purslane, ragweed, and plantain add to its chiefly grass seed menu. You'll often see this little bird freely hopping along the edges of walkways, gardens, and residential lawns picking up seeds and crumbs.

City and country bird. Aside from its urban-suburban visitations, the chipping sparrow appears commonly in sagebrush and desert fringes, streamsides, valleys, and hillsides on up to the upper level of pine forests.

White-crowned Sparrow

(Member of Finch-Sparrow-Grosbeak family)

ALL YEAR
SUMMER
WINTER

Although the nondescript gray and brown markings of many sparrows make them extremely difficult for the novice bird watcher to identify, the white-crowned sparrow is sure to attract the beginner's attention. Often regarded as the aristocrat of sparrows, this handsome bird regally wears a puffy crown of prominent black and white stripes which contrasts nicely with its pearly gray breast.

How to attract them. Seen during the winter months across the country, the white-crowned sparrow frequents roadsides, edges of woods, weedy fields, and backyard gardens. An open lawn with a shrubbery border is a perfect combination for attracting wintering flocks of sparrows. It allows them to forage for food on the ground but take refuge in nearby cover when disturbed. A flock can retreat so quickly that it often appears to move like a single bird.

Like other sparrows, the seed-eating white-crown probes for fallen seeds under shrubs and seed-producing annuals (California poppies, dandelions, forget-me-nots, and amaranths) that are left standing. Seasonal, wild fruits (such as the mulberry) are also eaten by the sparrow.

For supplementary winter feeding, scatter bird seed mixtures, bread crumbs, sunflower seeds, and nut-meats on the ground.

Young have brown stripes. While all adult white-crowns wear black and white head plumage (those of the female are slighter duller than the male's), subtle coloring differences occur in four varieties found in California. Young white-crowns have head stripes of light and dark brown.

Abundant in the West. Although white-crowns winter across most of the country, some are seen occasionally in the northeastern states during the colder months. White-crowns migrate as far north as the tundra of the Arctic region for breeding, but in the West they nest along the Pacific coast from the Sierra Nevadas and Rocky Mountains to Ventura, California and across to northern New Mexico. Western gardeners lucky enough to have the year-round company of white-crowns will notice that after flocking all winter, the sparrows pair off in spring in isolated nesting territories. The males will sing more than usual and will fight off rivals if necessary. White-crowns nest in shrubbery or on the ground and feed their nestlings a diet of insects, such as ants, beetles, caterpillars, and spiders.

Similar sparrows. In eastern gardens, the white-crown may be mistaken for the popular WHITE-THROATED SPARROW. Although the white-throat's crown is similar to that of the white-crown, it has a distinctive white throat patch and a yellow spot near each eye. Wintering from New England to the Gulf states (and sparsely in the West), the white-throat is a regular patron of grains or bread crumbs scattered on the ground. This migrant summers in Canada and the New England states.

In the Pacific states, the striking GOLDEN-CROWNED SPARROW often joins the white-crowns during the winter months, then heads into the northern mountains for the summer. A little larger but shyer and seen less frequently in gardens, the golden-crowns have a plaintive call with notes sounding like "oh dear me."

Song Sparrow

(Member of Finch-Sparrow-Grosbeak family)

■ ALL YEAR
▨ SUMMER
▨ WINTER

If it weren't for its delightful song, the very common but inconspicuous little brown song sparrow might not be noticed in your garden. Though its tune is not extraordinary, it is persistently sung year-round — day in, day out (and even during the darkness in between). Even in a rain storm, this songster will choose a prominent garden perch from which to pour out its song. But when the song sparrow is alarmed, you'll hear a metallic "cheep" and see the pumping of its long rounded tail as it heads for cover.

How to attract them. In the wild, song sparrows breed close to streams or marshes. If your garden has a birdbath or small pond, it may attract the sparrow. Loving a good splash, song sparrows reluctantly let other birds take their turn at cooling off.

For nesting, song sparrows choose a well-hidden spot on the ground, in a low bush, or in the tangled growth of honeysuckle, multiflora rose, or blackberry. They may even accept a nesting shelf nailed 1 to 3 feet above ground.

Although seed eaters primarily, song sparrows feed their young a rich diet of insects culled from the garden. Berry plants like blackberry, mulberry, and viburnums also attract song sparrows, and a variety of annuals can be left standing to offer seeds (amaranths, bachelor's buttons, cosmos, and California poppies).

Thicket-loving sparrows may become friendly enough to accept food in feeding trays, but they prefer a scattering of seeds (like hemp or millet) on the ground near cover. Other favorite foods are suet and peanut butter.

Many types. The song sparrow is one of the most adaptable of birds, inhabiting both fields and gardens. In the dry Southwest, they are smaller and lighter than northern birds of humid regions. More than 31 subspecies are recognized, differing in color and size. Each is marked by a heavily streaked breast with a dark splotch in the center.

Breed in the North. These cheerful songsters are found over most of the country, but they breed only in the northern states and Canada. Cold winter temperatures will cause song sparrows to retreat from the northern extremes and winter as far south as Mexico and the Gulf states. They live year-round over much of the West.

Shrubbery protects young. In the spring, song sparrows aggressively stake out their territories, normally keeping out intruding birds with a warning song but occasionally skirmishing over a chosen spot. After the males court the females with song, the birds pair off to raise a family. Since young song sparrows, like most ground birds, leave the nest before perfecting the art of flying, they require the cover of dense shrubbery in which to hide from roaming cats or other predators.

A varied song. Whether it's singing for the sake of singing or announcing its spring territory, the song sparrow varies its song endlessly. Thoreau described it as a warning — "Maids, maids, maids, hang up your teakettle, ettle, ettle." Another writer thought it sounded like "Hip, hip, hooray, boys, spring is here."

OCCASIONAL GARDEN VISITORS

Although most birds are attracted to environmental conditions that serve their basic needs, many birds will come to your garden even if the plantings and other provisions were not chosen specifically for them. The birds described below are some of the feathered guests who will drop by without invitation or notice. Of course, there are many others that belong to this group, but on a nationwide basis, we have selected some of the birds you are most likely to see.

Bobwhite. Member of Quail family. Shaped like a dumpy fat hen, the bobwhite calls its name "bob-bobwhite" in a loud whistle. This quail is commonly seen in eastern states (from southern Maine and South Dakota west to Arizona and the Gulf of Mexico). It frequents briar patches and thickets along the borders of fields and gardens. In the summer, the bobwhite eats insects while in the winter it feeds on a variety of fruits and waste grain found in the fields or around a garden. Although it's highly sought by game bird hunters, bobwhite is admired by many as a "singer."

California Quail. Member of Quail family. The main quail species in the West, the California quail is the official state bird of California. One of the most abundant and popular game birds, its striking feature is a drooping black top knot. Its desert relative, the Gambel's Quail, has the same adornment. Coveys or flocks of California quail are commonly seen on lawns and in gardens. It seeks protective cover in brush and thickets. Many kinds of seeds and fruits, especially grapes, are its main food sources.

Roadrunner. Member of Cuckoo family. A very familiar and picturesque desert resident, this large running bird with a foot-long tail is found in gardens and running along roadsides. It's a  shy bird that seldom flies and usually runs away rapidly to escape danger. Roadrunners feed on lizards, small snakes, crickets, grasshoppers, and a cafeteria selection of other small animal life.

Screech Owl. Member of the Owl family. A small owl, the screech owl resides in woodlands, orchards, small towns, and suburban areas. It nests in cavities of trees, especially abandoned nests of large woodpeckers—particularly the common flicker. It rarely nests in birdhouses.

The screech owl's varied diet largely consists of earthworms, moths, and grasshoppers along with fish, small birds, and mice. In the East, it is rufous-colored; the western version is grayish.

Yellow-bellied Sapsucker. Member of the Woodpecker family. The yellow-bellied sapsucker has a red face, a long white wing patch, and a mottled back. In the West, it sports an all-red head. An array of evenly-spaced small pits or holes in birch or poplar trees are probably the work of the sapsucker. It feeds on the inner bark of the trees, the sap, and the insects attracted to the sap. Mountain ash, alder, and many coniferous trees also serve as food sources.

Least Flycatcher. Member of the Flycatcher family. This bird is most likely to be seen east of the Rocky Mountains in a number of habitats. Cities and towns as well as open countrysides are common territories for this flycatcher. Its common name is "chebec" which it repeatedly calls out. Attracted to gardens, orchards, farms, shade trees, and parks, this bird's distinctive noisy voice is a better clue to its presence than its drab grayish green appearance. In typical flycatcher fashion, the least flycatcher sallies out from its perch to catch passing insects, then usually returns to the same perch.

Western Flycatcher. Member of the Flycatcher family. Widely distributed west of the Rockies, this bird seeks alders, maples, dogwoods, and other deciduous trees to provide the natural 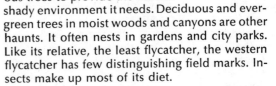 shady environment it needs. Deciduous and evergreen trees in moist woods and canyons are other haunts. It often nests in gardens and city parks. Like its relative, the least flycatcher, the western flycatcher has few distinguishing field marks. Insects make up most of its diet.

Brown Creeper. Member of Creeper family. Hard to see, this little brown bird creeps or hitches up a tree by spiraling around the trunk or branches. Subsequently, it flies to the base of another tree, repeating the pattern. Very few insects escape the brown creeper's intensive search. Suet in bird feeders attract these birds. It prefers dense-wooded areas but does associate with kinglets and chickadees in garden trees. Creepers are found throughout the country.

Brown Thrasher. Member of Mockingbird-Thrasher family. A large, brown, long-tailed bird, the brown thrasher should not be confused with the gray catbird or the mockingbird. Found in the East, it frequents tangled thickets and bushy borders, especially around homes and gardens. In spring and fall, it visits birdbaths and feeders. Although insects make up the bulk of its food, thrashers also eat berries and acorns.

Hermit Thrush. Member of Thrush family. Commonly mistaken for the fox sparrow, the hermit thrush has a rusty-colored tail and body. Its slender bill is in contrast to the shorter, heavier bill of the fox sparrow. Scratching for food on the ground is not one of the thrush's habits. Instead it searches for insects among leafy litter. Berries are also sought, especially from the western toyon. The hermit thrush has a wide range of habitat adaptation. In winter it will frequent garden paths, corridors, and feeders.

Swainson's Thrush. Member of Thrush family. Similar to the hermit thrush, the Swainson's thrush's distinctive markings are buffy or light tan face parts and breast. It, too, sings melodiously, but its song does not compare with the richness of the hermit thrush song. Although it prefers the mature, coniferous forests of the North, this bird is also common in moist lowlands with mixed growth. It will visit gardens with damp and shady shrubbery. Although insects are the thrush's staple food, it also enjoys wild fruit.

Red-eyed Vireo. Member of Vireo family. A tireless, persistent singer with a "conversational style," the red-eyed vireo is found wherever there are trees—in gardens, parks, streets, and woodlands. It's widespread in its geographical distribution but only occasionally appears in Utah, California, Arizona, and western Texas. Insects dominate the vireo's summer menu. In the fall it eats various kinds of berries and the fruits of sassafras and magnolia trees.

Warbling Vireo. Member of Vireo family. Although it has pale gray nondescript coloring, the warbling vireo possesses a loud distinctive warbling song. During nesting season, the sing- ing is nearly a non-stop affair — several thousand songs a day is the normal frequency. Typically this insect-eater inhabits the upper foliage of willows, cottonwoods, elms, and other shade trees.

Palm Warbler. Member of Wood Warbler family. Sometimes called the "tip-up" warbler, the palm warbler seems to keep time by incessantly wagging its tail. Large numbers of these yel- low-breasted and brown-capped birds winter in Florida palms, gardens, and fields where they may be one of the most common birds. Occasionally it spends the winter in the North where it visits feeders and birdbaths. In the summer this warbler abides in northern woodlands in the eastern half of the country and parts of Canada.

Western Tanager. Member of Tanager family. A strikingly beautiful bird of the western coniferous forests, the male western tanager has a bright red head, yellow body, black tail, and white bars on its wings. During spring migration, the birds wander through gardens, parks, and orchards eating fruit, berries, and seeds.

Scarlet Tanager. Member of Tanager family. The handsomely attractive scarlet tanager is found in the East. The male bird has fiery red body plumage with solid jet black wings and tail. Normally found in a woodland environment, the tanager feeds on insects in tree tops. Occasionally this bird will visit a garden for food or a birdbath. It especially savors caterpillars.

Pine Siskin. Member of Finch-Sparrow-Grosbeak family. A cousin of the goldfinch, the pine siskin looks like a brown-streaked goldfinch with yellow bars on the wings. It prefers conifers in high altitudes as its breeding habitat. In winter, siskins scatter over the northern half of the United States feeding on the seeds and winter buds of birch and alder. Fruits of the willow, alder, and sycamore are its chief foods in spring and fall.

Fox Sparrow. Member of Finch-Sparrow-Grosbeak family. The fox sparrow is a large sparrow with a brownish red tail and heavy streaked patterns on its breast. The body plumage of 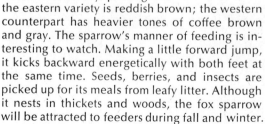 the eastern variety is reddish brown; the western counterpart has heavier tones of coffee brown and gray. The sparrow's manner of feeding is interesting to watch. Making a little forward jump, it kicks backward energetically with both feet at the same time. Seeds, berries, and insects are picked up for its meals from leafy litter. Although it nests in thickets and woods, the fox sparrow will be attracted to feeders during fall and winter.

Supplementary Feeding and Care

HOUSE FINCHES ENJOY FEEDER STOCKED WITH SEEDS; BATH IS AT LEFT.

Although you can plant trees, shrubs, vines, and ground covers (see pages 48-93) in your garden to provide birds with food and shelter, the job may not end there. At certain times of the year, some birds will appreciate supplementary food in addition to a regular water supply.

Why give supplementary feeding?

If you set out young plants and then sit back eagerly awaiting the arrival of thankful birds, you're bound to be disappointed. It will be several years before the new plants are large enough to provide food and shelter. Until then, birds will be attracted only to the food and water you furnish. They will seek shelter elsewhere. Even after the plants are fully grown, you can attract a greater number of birds to your garden with additional food.

In regions where winter temperatures often fall below freezing, supplementary feeding can help guarantee that birds will survive the long winter months. Remember, however, that birds quickly become accustomed to handouts in one spot, and if your feeder is empty for just one day, numerous birds could die. Even if they are sheltered, birds need enough daily food to keep their metabolic rate high enough to generate body warmth during frigid nights.

During summer and fall, the natural growth of your garden plants usually produces ample food for most visiting birds. But no matter how well the plants do their job, they can't always attract birds to spots where you can see them best. Strategically placed feeders can. Of course, feeder types and placement involve some do's and don'ts (see pages 41-42), but you'll probably have no trouble finding a good location near a window where you can view the passing feathered parade.

WHAT BIRDS EAT

Although the categories sometimes overlap, the eating habits of birds generally can be divided into two groups: a diet primarily of insects and other small organisms, and a diet mainly of seeds.

Every established garden has some insects to attract birds. Those gardens that are sprayed the least with pesticides will naturally offer more insect life. A few plants can be planted as a lure for insects. A good example is the birch. It often harbors a sizable spring aphid population and then goes on to produce a good seed crop in the fall.

Nationwide, the various sparrows probably are the most familiar seed eaters. In spring and summer they and their short and broad-billed brethren are satisfied naturally by the countless tons of seed produced each year by garden weeds, flowers, shrubs, and trees. To supplement their diet in winter, you only need to buy some seeds and put them in your feeder.

Some birds have been known to eat an amazing variety of foods. Kitchen scraps of almost every imaginable kind have been gobbled up by grateful birds not only in periods of natural food shortages but even when food is plentiful. But before considering this type of menu, here are the more basic foods you can buy.

Suet. A favorite year-round food of insect eaters is beef suet (the all-fat trimmings from meat). Suet is a quick energy source and helps to keep birds' metabolisms high enough to produce body warmth even in cold weather. In spring and summer months, it's a luxury item, but in freezing temperatures it may be a necessity if you want a large number of birds to stay around.

The simplest way to provide suet is to set it out in chunk form. The bigger the chunks, the better. Small birds will peck away until they are satisfied. Larger, aggressive birds won't be able to fly off with large chunks. As an overall precaution against bigger birds carrying away more than their share of suet, many people cover it with ½-inch wire mesh. Birds of all sizes can peck through the wire but get only small pieces of suet. Ready-made wire mesh suet feeders are sold by bird equipment dealers. Before you buy one,

Wire mesh container *holds suet; hairy woodpecker can cling to mesh or use the chopstick perches.*

however, be sure it's not made of collapsible wire mesh. Birds' feet could become entangled in the flexible metal and become severely damaged.

String or fiber mesh bags (those often used for oranges or onions) also make a good suet container. Some garden or pet supply shops sell mesh bags especially made for bird feeding.

Another type of suet feeder can be made with small logs (see page 40). Drill one-inch diameter holes into (but not through) the log, filling each hole with melted suet. When the suet hardens, hang the log from a tree limb. If the log has a rough surface, it may be visited by any of the birds — such as nuthatches — that are able to cling to a tree trunk. To attract other birds, insert a small wood dowel about an inch below some of the holes to act as a perch.

Instead of making or buying any of the suet feeders described here, some people prefer to make suet cakes and place or hang them wherever possible. Simply melt the suet and pour it into any container that has outward flaring sides (this enables you to remove the hardened cake). If you want to hang the cake, hold a stick or string upright in the center of the mold until the suet begins to harden.

Peanut butter. Like suet, peanut butter is a good high energy food. It also provides some quantities of salt which birds need. But when used alone, peanut butter can cake in the mouths of some birds so badly that they are prevented from eating anything else. To guard against this possibility, mix the peanut butter with equal parts of corn meal or enough to make the consistency somewhat granular. Place it on a feeding tray (see page 41) or in suet logs (see page 40) or spread small patches of it onto trunks of rough-barked trees.

Seeds. Pet shops, feed stores, and many supermarkets sell bird seed — often in mixtures called "wild bird

Suet log *hangs from pine branch; wood dowels form perches. Pine cone at left has covering of suet.*

Mixture of seeds *awaits arrival of hungry birds. Branch attached to feeder is handy landing site.*

seed." The mixtures usually contain a number of different kinds and quantities of seeds known to be liked by a variety of birds. These easily available seed mixtures are an inducement to begin feeding and to continue on a regular basis. Using seed mixtures as supplementary food has no particular disadvantages, but you might want to consider these points before buying any: 1) Pound for pound, mixed seeds may be the most costly of all bird seed on the market, especially when bought in small packages. 2) Not all seeds in the mixture may be preferred equally by the birds in your garden. 3) Most pet shops and some feed stores sell separate types of seed by the pound. Bird enthusiasts have devised a simple way to determine birds' preferences. Construct a feeding tray (see page 41) and temporarily section it off into equal-sized areas. Then fill each section with measured amounts of the various seeds you want to test. Those that are eaten first are the ones you should put out in your feeder.

Keep in mind that some mixtures contain sunflower seeds that appeal to a number of desirable garden birds. But they are also liked by aggressive jays. If you have jays in your neighborhood, consider setting up a separate feeding station for them a good distance from your primary feeder. If you stock it with sunflower seeds, it's likely the jays will prefer that feeder.

Fruits, berries, nuts. During summer, fall, and early winter, these food items usually are provided by nature — especially in suburban and country areas. But from midwinter on, in cold-winter regions, this supply rapidly diminishes. Raisins, dried currants, and any other dried fruit (cut into small pieces) will be welcome meals. Fresh fruit, cut into manageable hunks, is also good. Although some nuts are costly, they help keep a bird's metabolism rate fairly high. Peanuts and walnuts are the least expensive.

Kitchen scraps. Many leftovers are similar to the food birds find in gardens. For example, nearly all forms of baked goods — bread, cake, doughnuts, stale cookies — will be eagerly gobbled up. Although not the most nutritious food, they do provide salt required by birds.

The same is true with crumbled crackers and potato chips. Even the grains we eat — rice and corn, for example — are palatable to birds.

For the insect eaters, try setting out pieces of cheese, bacon scraps, diced raw meat, or dry dog food. In the spring, any of these items will be highly nutritious — especially for young birds still in the nest. Be careful to make the pieces small enough so that the parent birds can carry them away easily.

Birds also like some leftover fruits and vegetables. It's just a matter of experimenting to see what they like best.

If you would like to attract birds to a spot where you can watch them eat, the pieces of food should be so large that birds can't carry them away or so small that they'll be eaten on the spot. Or you can put the food in mesh enclosures or bags described under "Suet" (see page 39).

Other foods. Many bird enthusiasts have found chicken feed to be as appealing to birds as are seeds and present it in the same way. Cracked corn also is popular with many seed eaters.

Fresh coconut in the shell is another recommended food for birds. *Be careful not to use shredded coconut; it swells in birds' stomachs.* From half a coconut shell, you can make a hanging feeder. Birds will perch on the shell while they eat the coconut meat.

One easily overlooked part of a bird's diet is nonedible roughage, commonly called *grit.* Although this may sound unappetizing, sand particles, crushed shells, bits of old mortar, or other similar materials help grind the food in the birds' stomachs and provide useful minerals. In the northeastern states, for example, soils often are lacking in calcium. Even though you'll see birds in this region finding ample food, they still may be deficient in this important mineral. By including crushed clam or oyster shells (or even crushed egg shells) on your feeding table, you can help compensate for the lack of calcium. Crushed shells and other kinds of grit are sold by some pet shops, specialty bird supply stores, and feed stores.

THE FEEDING TABLE

The phrase "setting the table" is more apt for birds than you might first imagine. Known to many bird enthusiasts as a "feeding table," the most basic bird feeder is an elevated flat surface. It can be simple or quite elaborate in design — within the bounds of what attracts birds. Here and on the next page you will find several suggestions for feeder design, as well as construction tips and guidelines for best placement in the garden.

Types to choose from

Basically there are four types of feeding tables. Your choice will depend largely upon the character of your garden and the kind of feeding table (or tables) it will accommodate best.

Platform atop a post. The simplest type of table is 4½ to 6 feet above ground, putting the table beyond a cat's leap, yet low enough so that shrubbery and ground-feeding birds will come to it. Birds are wary creatures — always on guard against sudden, swift predators (typified by cats and hawks). They will shy away from feeders placed in bushes or under a thick-ly foliaged overhanging branch because the denseness could conceal "the enemy." A feeding site near shrubbery (anywhere from 8 to 20 feet away) is an ideal location. Birds like a spot close at hand where they can take cover. Placed near shrubs and trees that dissipate the wind's bite, your feeding table will be more popular than would the same model placed in the open. Take care never to place your feeder too close to a wood fence or flat-topped wall; both can serve as handy launching pads for cats. About 8 feet from either structure is as close as you can safely position a feeder.

Ground-level feeding station. This feeder requires even closer attention to the same "rules" for placement than the elevated table. At its simplest, the ground station can be no more than a cleared spot of earth. With a little added ingenuity it can be an attractive deck or patio smorgasbord (see photograph on page 38). Because it is on the ground — or so close to it — it's especially important not to place it near cat-hiding places, such as tall grass or dense shrubs. If you live in the country or outlying suburbs, your feeder may attract the ground-feeding game birds: quail, pheasants, and doves.

Windowsills. Widely used as feeding tables, the windowsill can be comfortably used by most birds. The

---

HOW TO CONSTRUCT A FEEDING TABLE

In little more than the time it takes you to dig a hole for the post, you can construct a simple feeding table. Because the construction is so easy, you might as well take a little more time to add a few niceties that will make the platform safer for the birds to use and relatively easy for you to maintain.

The type of supporting pole or post you use will make it easier or more difficult for cats to reach the feeder. A metal pole is foolproof. A wooden post, on the other hand, can be somewhat risky if several cats live in the neighborhood. Either one of two metal devices affixed to the post can foil any cat that begins to climb it. One is a metal sheath, at least 18 inches wide, securely fastened around the post at a point high enough to keep a cat from leaping above it. Less attractive is a metal cone attached just below the table, its larger opening (about 18 inches in diameter) facing down. This is similar to rat guards you see on ships' mooring ropes.

Once you've taken care of these safety precautions, consider some of the refinements you can add to the basic platform for your benefit and that of the birds. Most important is to make sure the table has some drainage provisions so that food won't become waterlogged and spoiled during rainy seasons. You can use any number of methods to take care of water runoff, but if the table is made of wood, the following simple solution solves both water runoff and spoilage problems. A feeding table should have raised edges to keep food from spilling and blowing off. When you put on the edges, leave a small gap at each corner through which excess water will drain out.

Don't skimp on the size of the table. Ideally it should be in the 3 to 4-square-foot range. This is large enough for a number of birds to visit at one time. A 2-foot-square table gives you a 4-square-foot feeding surface; 18 inches by 2 feet makes a 3-square-foot table.

Although most birds prefer to have open sky above them while they feed, you may want to add a roof to your table if you live in a frequently rainy or snowy region. If your feeder is enclosed, you'll have to remove the roof in order to replace the food. A compromise solution is to roof only the part of the table where you dispense the food; leave the other part open so birds can carry larger bits of food there for eating. If you decide not to add a roof, consider using a seed hopper or dispenser. They dispense only a small amount of seed at a time — as the birds consume it. In snow country, though, only a roofed feeder will keep you from having to scrape off snow.

sill should be on the side of your house opposite prevailing winds. Nearly all ground-story windowsills are a good height for bird feeding. Again, be sure to select a window that is not surrounded by dense shrubbery or luxuriant, woody vines.

Hanging food tables. Attractive and inviting, hanging food tables can be hung in tall, stout-limbed trees or simply from a wire strung between two trees or between a house and tree or pole in the garden. But the feeders should hang only 5 to 6 feet above the ground, should have relatively clear ground underneath (groundcovers or low annuals and perennials are fine, but no bushes), and must be as far from cat-concealing vegetation as any of the other feeders.

Presenting the food

Like man, birds are creatures of habit. Because most are cautious, some time may elapse before your bird banquet table is discovered and used. But once it is, the birds will expect it to be set at all times. (The need for maintaining a constant winter supply is explained on pages 38-39.)

A steady food supply. The success of your bird feeder depends entirely on you. Unless you keep the feeders regularly stocked, you won't have a steady, faithful stream of visitors. With occasional feeding you may always attract the most common and sometimes unwanted, aggressive birds (house sparrows, starlings, jays, to name a few), but you'll see other types only occasionally. If there's no food in the feeder when birds stop by, they're not going to stay around.

Just as important as a steady food supply is making sure that it's available every day at the times when the birds make their routine visits. Putting out food one day at 8 A.M., the next day at noon, and continuing on in a similarly erratic pattern will just confuse the birds — especially if the amount is small enough to be consumed during one day. The best approach is to set out the food as early in the morning as you can. That's the time when birds need to refuel as a result of the night's weight and water loss.

Vary the food. You also might give thought to varying (on a seasonal basis) the food you offer. During winter birds' greatest need is for high-energy foods such as suet, peanut butter, meat scraps, and nuts. As the weather grows warmer this need decreases and often can be satisfied by what nature provides in insects and high-calorie seeds and nuts. During the nesting season and until the young birds become fully grown, don't offer much bread or other bakery scraps. They are less nutritious than other foods.

Dealing with aggressive birds. One feeding problem you're likely to puzzle over is how to keep away the really pushy, greedy birds in order to give others a sporting chance to get their share of food. Having more than one feeder is one solution. If your area hosts many jays, place a second feeder a good distance away from the first and stock it with sunflower seeds.

If the pushy birds are house sparrows and starlings, and if your feeder is near a window of your house, a few sharp raps on the windowpane will scare them away. Because it will be the same local groups of these birds that will try to visit your feeder all season, several successive scares should get the message across.

A second method of dealing with sparrows and starlings is based on their preferred mode of eating: both are ground feeders. If you select an open location (not

Projecting roof supports *on diamond-shaped feeder provide a perch for birds. Roof, bottom tray are constructed of overlapping shingles.*

Tiered feeder *is made of wood salad bowls glued to dowels inserted in pole.*

Come on in — *the water's fine. Blackbird bathes in an inch of water; bath floor has rough surface.*

Concrete birdbath *is shallow at one end, deeper at opposite end. Spray from hose is added enticement.*

too near shrubbery) away from your primary feeder and regularly scatter food on the ground, the starlings and sparrows are likely to prefer this feeding station to any elevated spot. (For added information on coping with unwanted birds, see page 24.)

A WATERING STATION

What's a meal without a beverage? A bird's answer would be "incomplete." And in their case, the preferred liquid is water. Regardless of the weather, birds need daily access to water. In regions where it snows, much of this requirement may be satisfied by whatever snow adheres to their food, but even then an unfrozen "watering hole" will be nearly as popular as a feeding station. In desert and other semi-arid regions, water may prove even more popular during the hot season than will a feeding station.

Birds also must have water to bathe in. You'll see them cavorting in a shallow body of water, splashing it all over themselves and anything else nearby. Some of this activity may be pure sport, but it is also part of a cleaning ritual in which their feathers are meticulously preened and cleaned.

Drawing the bath

Despite birds' basic attraction to water, you won't lure them to a birdbath if it has steep sides and deep water. For bathing, the water must be contained so that birds can wade out to a comfortable depth. If it's necessary for birds to plunge in from high sides, you'll only get drinkers perching around the edge.

For maximum effectiveness the bath must provide gradual transition from very shallow to deeper water

— no more than a 3-inch depth at the deepest. It could be a broad, shallow bowl in which deep water is in the center. Or you could provide a swimming pool-like bath where one end is shallow, the other deep. The gradual deepening of water — from about ½ inch to 3 inches — will let any garden bird find a satisfactory depth.

The material you use to make a bath is not important as long as the bottom of the bath is not porcelain smooth. Birds need a slightly rough-textured surface in order to maintain a good foothold.

The best way to lure birds to water is to have running water — whether it is just a simple "drip, drip" as though from a leaky faucet, or a fountainlike spray.

Location and care

The basic guidelines for feeder location also apply to a birdbath: place it near shrubbery where birds can fly to safety but not so close that a lurking cat could have easy pickings. This is especially important for ground level baths; a wet bird is slower moving and more vulnerable than when dry.

Your bird watering station will need frequent refilling. Once the birds discover the water, they'll expect to find it there regularly. An erratic water supply means erratic numbers of bird visitors.

A periodic cleaning of the water basin is also important.

Birds' need for water doesn't diminish in wintertime. In cold-winter climates, this means keeping the water unfrozen at least part of the time.

If you prefer to let nature take care of thawing the ice, locate the basin of water in a spot where winter sun strikes most of the day. To help nature along just a bit, nothing has replaced the age-old tradition of using hot water to melt a frozen birdbath.

How to Beat the Housing Shortage

SWALLOW FAMILY LIVES IN THIS BIRDHOUSE. DIMENSIONS CAN BE ALTERED FOR OTHER BIRDS.

It may come as a surprise, but birds can suffer from housing shortages, particularly in recently developed suburban areas where new gardens have not grown enough to provide desirable nesting sites. In plantless urban sites and in overly manicured suburban gardens, the situation also may be difficult.

Even rural farmland is not always hospitable; as woods are cut, brush cleared, and tree crops better cared for, the number of nesting areas is reduced. The seriousness of the housing shortage is exemplified by what happened to the eastern bluebird. Favoring cavities in old trees for making their nests, these birds were driven farther and farther away from civilization as modern agriculture grew healthier trees and patched up or removed old, decaying ones.

The answer to the birds' problem — and a means by which to lure birds to your garden — is to offer them man-made housing. No elaborate work is required to build an adequate birdhouse, but you'll have to observe certain "building codes" in order to make sure that your newly provided homes will be eagerly occupied by the birds you want (see below).

Birds can be discriminating about their accommodations. A particular species won't nest in just any box with a hole in one side. The box must be within a particular size range, and the hole a certain height from the floor and of a particular diameter. For example, there's no point in putting out a shoe-box-sized structure with a 2-inch hole to attract wrens. They simply won't use it — it's too large to be cozy and the 2-inch opening will allow other larger birds to enter and threaten the occupants.

Before you even pick up a hammer and nails, you should know what birds are likely to nest in your area. Then you can construct housing that will have a good chance of appealing to them. The chart below lists some familiar garden birds that will nest in man-made houses and gives specifications for their needs in house size, diameter of opening, and its height from the house's floor.

Not all birds will use birdhouses — another good reason for knowing what birds frequent your part of the country. Swallows, for example, make their nests on open ledges, often just under the eaves of buildings. For ledge nesters, you need only to provide a nesting shelf such as the ones illustrated on page 47.

NESTING BOX DIMENSIONS

Dimensions of nesting boxes for various species of birds that regularly use them, and the height at which they should be placed above the ground.

Species	Floor of Cavity	Depth of Cavity	Entrance above Floor	Diameter of Entrance	Height above Ground[1]
	Inches	Inches	Inches	Inches	Feet
House finch	5x5	8	6	1½	5–10
Robin	6x8	8	(2)	(2)	6–15
Black-capped chickadee	4x4	8–10	6–8	1⅛	6–15
Tufted titmouse	4x4	8–10	6–8	1¼	6–15
Nuthatch	4x4	8–10	6–8	1¼	12–20
House wren	4x4	6–8	1–6	1–1¼	6–10
Bewick's wren	4x4	6–8	1–6	1–1¼	6–10
Carolina wren	4x4	6–8	1–6	1½	6–10
Violet-green swallow	5x5	6	1–5	1½	10–15
Tree swallow	5x5	6	1–5	1½	10–15
Barn swallow	6x6	6	(2)	(2)	8–12
Purple martin	6x6	6	1	2½	15–20
Starling	6x6	16–18	14–16	2	10–25
Black and eastern phoebe	6x6	6	(2)	(2)	8–12
Common flicker	7x7	16–18	14–16	2½	6–20
Red-headed woodpecker	6x6	12–15	9–12	2	12–20
Downy woodpecker	4x4	9–12	6–8	1¼	6–20
Hairy woodpecker	6x6	12–15	9–12	1½	12–20
Screech owl	8x8	12–15	9–12	3	10–30

[1] Many experiments show that boxes at moderate heights mostly within reach of a man on the ground are readily accepted by many birds.

[2] One or more sides open.

All three of these easy-to-build birdhouses are constructed in the same way (see sketch below).

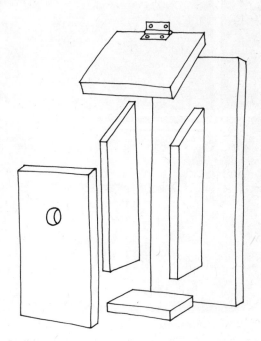

Dimensions for birdhouses in photo above can be varied for different birds; hinged roof lifts up to make regular cleaning of the house easier.

Condominium for birds that don't mind close quarters; these box-style birdhouses hang on dowels pushed through holes in a tall redwood post. Although only two boxes are shown here, you can make several and hang them from all four sides of the post. The dimensions given in the sketch (see below) will make a comfortable home for purple martins. All parts were nailed together; top, sides, and bottom were cut to 45° miters (butt-joining the ends of the boards would be easier). Fasten one of the sides with only a couple of nails so you can remove it for easy cleaning. If you plan to leave the wood unpainted, choose redwood or cedar. Design: Donald Wm. MacDonald, AIA.

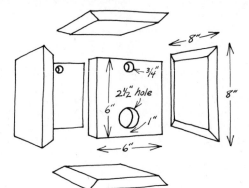

Ghost town birdhouses were made from weathered boards, fence laths, and furniture scraps. Small drain holes in the floors let out any rain that gets in. Use only a few nails to attach one side of each roof so that it can be easily removed for cleaning. Design: Hugh Wayne.

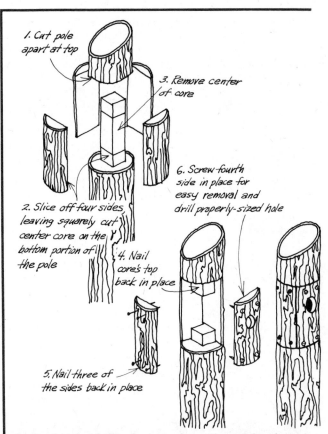

1. Cut pole apart at top

2. Slice off four sides, leaving squarely cut center core on the bottom portion of the pole

3. Remove center of core

4. Nail core's top back in place

5. Nail three of the sides back in place

6. Screw fourth side in place for easy removal and drill properly-sized hole

Natural pole birdhouse (popular with woodpeckers) is like a hollow tree trunk. Follow carefully the steps given in sketch. Design: Donald Wm. MacDonald, AIA.

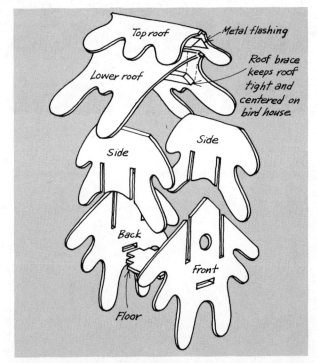

Slide together *all pieces but the roof. The roof has six parts: a block holding it firmly in place, two large lower-roof panels, a short strip of sheet-metal flashing to keep the rain out, and two top panels. Nail all of the roof pieces together using rustproof nails.*

Surrealistic tree *is the shape this birdhouse takes. Although a relatively untested design, it could be popular with wrens or woodpeckers. Care to experiment first? Design: Donald Wm. MacDonald, AIA.*

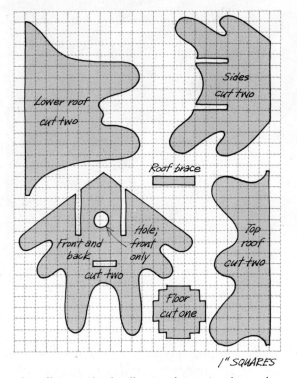

Cutting diagram *for birdhouse shown in photo above shows the shapes to cut from 3⁄8" exterior plywood. Sizes will depend upon the birds you'd like to attract (see Nesting Box Dimensions, page 45).*

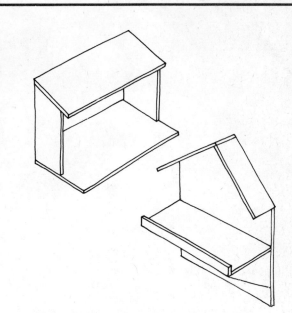

Nesting shelves, *popular with robins and barn swallows, allow observation of birds' activities. The two shelves shown above were designed to hang from a wall that is partially protected from the elements.*

Plants Birds Like the Most

BROWN TOWHEE CHECKS RIPENESS OF A FIG.

If your garden is "squeaky clean," it's not for the birds. The gardener who is constantly raking, pruning, mowing, and spraying for pests will find that his garden fails to attract and hold a variety of garden birds. To catch a bird's attention, a garden should provide a more natural environment — one that has not been too carefully groomed. But don't assume that a natural-looking garden means an unkempt one. Usually it indicates a garden in which healthy or hardy plants have been chosen, then arranged so they can grow without restrictive pruning.

All birds need food, cover, and nesting sites in order to survive. But the daily requirements may differ from one species to another. A garden most likely to fill all of these needs is full of variety — variety in types, numbers, and arrangement of plants. For example, a lawn surrounded by a few amply crowned trees, clumps of berry-producing shrubbery, luxuriant ground cover, and a tangled thicket of vines could easily satisfy a robin looking for insects, fruit, and a tree crotch for nesting. Other happy guests might be song sparrows or towhees, content with seeds to eat and shrubbery in which to build their nests.

This chapter shows you how the careful selection of plants and subsequent planting can meet the food and shelter requirements of most birds.

HOW TO PROVIDE FOOD

The insect-eating chickadee, seed-eating house finch, and berry-loving mockingbird all depend on vegetation for their food supply. In order to keep all three types as part of your constant bird population, you must make sure that your garden provides ample food in all seasons of the year.

Generally, garden supplies of insects, fruits, and seeds remain abundant in most regions from spring throughout the summer and into early fall. But in areas with cold-winter climates or low seasonal temperatures, late winter and early spring can be critical times for birds that don't migrate southward to milder, all-year climates. During these seasons, insects, fruits, and seeds are scarce.

Plants that bear fruits and berries

Because of the shortage of food in the coldest season, your garden plan should include some of the trees and shrubs that bear fruits and berries late into winter. Some of the better known of these plants include the barberry, bayberry, bush honeysuckle, cotoneaster, crabapple, hawthorn, holly, juniper, mahonia, mountain ash, and Virginia creeper. In early fall when other food is still plentiful, birds may leave these plants alone because their fruits tend to be either hard or very sour. In early spring when rising temperatures soften these fruits, and other food becomes scarce, the same plants provide a welcome emergency larder. Plants that bear edible fruit into late winter are noted in the special feature on page 51.

In cold climates, even though you may select plants to provide a winter food supply, you might want to supply additional provisions at a backyard feeding station. See pages 39-40 for the types of food to provide and pages 41-42 for ideas on types of feeders.

Fortunately for the gardener, many of the fruiting trees, shrubs, and vines that attract hungry birds are also attractive landscape subjects. Just a few examples of these doubly valuable plantings are the dogwoods, hawthorns, crabapples, mahonias, cherries, viburnums, and honeysuckles.

When you're choosing locations for berry and fruit-producing plants, remember that soft, fleshy fruits and berries can drop to the ground and cause an objectionable litter and/or staining problem.

Plants that attract insects

Although most gardeners don't react to insect life on garden plants with much enthusiasm, they realize that

Fennel seeds *entice a young sparrow. This plant is one of the wild "weeds" that seed eaters favor.*

insects attract birds. Many birds are almost wholly insect eating, busily exploring every nook and cranny of your yard. Their search is extensive. A black-capped chickadee may cling to outer branches of a conifer or deciduous tree, carefully picking around for insects and their eggs. A downy woodpecker spirals up tree trunks or along branches, inspecting the bark and poking into it for burrowing insect life. Nuthatches comb the same territory often in a downward direction. In a lawn, mockingbirds and robins eye the ground for worms.

Other birds known to eat such garden pests as beetles, slugs, cutworms, mosquitoes, and caterpillars include titmice, bushtits, wrens, waxwings, kinglets, warblers, and orioles. In order to feed their young, all birds must catch enormous quantities of insects.

Birds alone won't completely eliminate insects from your garden (nor will you). But the presence of numerous birds should help keep the insect and pest populations down to reasonable amounts.

Plants that produce seeds

Sparrows, goldfinches, house finches, and juncos will avidly eat the seeds of weedy plants, such as plantain, dock, thistle, goldenrod, fennel, and wild grasses. But only gardeners with large properties might allow themselves the luxury of an out-of-the-way weed patch that will attract birds. An alternative to weed seeds is to let garden flowers go to seed after blooming. If you grow seasonal flowers, this method will provide some food in summer, fall, and winter. Flowers that have attractive blossoms followed by tasty seeds include amaranth, aster, bachelor's button, columbine, coreopsis, forget-me-not, poppy (particularly California poppy), phlox, sunflower, and zinnia. Because sunflower seeds are excellent additions to feeding tables (see page 40), you might want to use a small patch of your garden for growing these mammoth yellow flowers.

Large trees also attract seed-eating birds. Eagerly sought after are seeds from ashes, maples, elms, tulip trees, and sycamores. The small, seed-bearing catkins of birches and alders and the larger conifer cones will provide food for many birds. Oak acorns are picked up by jays, woodpeckers, and nuthatches to supplement their main diet of insects.

PROVIDING FOR SHELTER AND NESTING

In addition to providing natural food for birds, the foliage and growth of some garden plants can offer birds shelter against the elements, protective cover from enemies, and even a spot to set up housekeeping.

A garden with a variety of plants will provide adequate shelter and cover for most birds. But to keep a bird happily settled in your yard, a few plants must also satisfy some specific nesting site requirements (see next column).

Sheltering plants

A thick stand of coniferous evergreen trees creates the best year-round shield against wind, rain, or snow — particularly in regions where winter temperatures fall below zero. Wherever it grows successfully, a top choice would be a hemlock hedge. If this doesn't fit

Forked branch with three "prongs" (stems) offers safe anchorage for this sturdy flycatcher's nest.

into your garden scheme, many of the pines and spruces suited to your region would do just as well. In cold climates, you'll often find a large group of one bird species roosting together on a limb of any one of these trees. Where winter temperature drop is less severe, any group of other dense, broad-leafed evergreen trees, shrubs, or vines will protect birds from rain and driving wind. The special feature on the next page suggests some of the best choices.

Protective and concealing plants

A variety of trees and undergrowth can offer birds protective cover or completely hide them. Just about the best protection against possible enemies is an overgrown thicket, tangle, or "wild jungle" of shrubs and vines. Such a conglomeration of plants won't always be the most attractive landscape subject, but it's a good choice for an out-of-the-way spot in the yard — a back corner or area between the garage and fence. A few good candidates for creating this kind of protective cover are honeysuckle, bittersweet, multiflora rose, and wild blackberry. Thorns are no obstacle to the entry of a bird into the tangle, but they generally stop a dog or cat.

If a naturalistic protective tangle of shrubs and vines won't fit into your garden plans, you might consider planting a hedge or a mixed shrub border around the edge of your yard or lawn. As a hiding place, it's just as effective as a tangled thicket. But unless the shrubs are spiny, the protection from predators may not be quite as good. Another consideration is that, where a shrub border fronts a lawn, the plants nearest the lawn should branch low to the ground, providing smooth transition from grass to higher vegetation.

Nesting plants

Shelter for a nesting site is particularly critical. Foliage must keep out any hot sun or chilling rain and must hide the nest from nest-robbing predators (including certain other birds).

But a bird's choice of a nesting site is not determined only by the amount of cover available. In selecting a sturdy nesting foundation, each species has its definite preferences for branch height above the ground, forked limbs, or tree crotches.

A garden without evergreen and deciduous trees, shrubby underbrush, thicket, or protected ground cover won't attract potential nesters. Most bird species will not change their nesting preferences to suit the available vegetation in your yard. A ground-nesting brown towhee, for example, will build its nest wherever it finds suitable ground rather than stay in a garden that has only trees or shrubs.

Tree-nesting garden birds generally choose spots at forking branches or tree crotches that are firm enough to hold the nest's weight and are between 5 and 15 feet above the ground. To insure nesting privacy, ground and shrub-nesting birds need a border or thicket 3 to 10 feet high and at least 6 feet wide (preferably wider).

The hedge also works as a shrub border. It will offer nesting sites if the plants (such as hawthorns) produce

PRIME FAVORITE PLANTS

Even though all plants described in this section are sure to be appreciated by at least some birds, there are some plants especially preferred or that are used by a great variety of birds. For easy reference, check this listing for the prime favorite plants in various categories.

FRUITS

Amelanchier (Shadbush)
Cornus (Dogwood)
Crataegus (Hawthorn)
Heteromeles (Toyon)
Ilex (Holly)
Lindera (Spicebush)
Lonicera (Honeysuckle)
Malus (Crabapple)
Myrica (Bayberry)
Prunus (Cherry, Plum)
Pyracantha (Firethorn)
Rubus (Blackberry, Raspberry)
Sorbus (Mountain ash)
Vaccinium (Blueberry)
Viburnum (Viburnum)

SEEDS (woody plants)

Acer (Maple)
Alnus (Alder)
Betula (Birch)
Euonymus (Euonymus)
Fraxinus (Ash)

INSECTS

Acer (Maple)
Betula (Birch)

Platanus (Sycamore, Plane tree)
Salix (Willow)
Ulmus (Elm)

WINTER FRUITS

Celtis occidentalis (Common hackberry)
Crataegus phaenopyrum (Washington thorn)
Elaeagnus angustifolia (Russian olive)
Ilex glabra, I. opaca (Inkberry, American holly)
Juniperus virginiana (Eastern red cedar)
Liriodendron tulipifera (Tulip tree)
Lonicera maackii (Amur honeysuckle)
Malus sargentii (Sargent crabapple)
Myrica pensylvanica (Bayberry)
Phellodendron amurense (Amur cork tree)
Rosa multiflora (Multiflora or Japanese rose)
Rhus glabra, R. typhina (Smooth sumac, Staghorn sumac)
Sorbus americana, S. aucuparia (American mountain ash, European mountain ash)
Viburnum opulus, V. trilobum (European cranberry bush, American cranberry bush)

SHELTER AND COVER

Abies (Fir)
Berberis (Barberry)
Juniperus (Juniper)
Ligustrum (Privet)
Lonicera tatarica (Tatarian honeysuckle)
Lycium (Matrimony vine)
Morus (Mulberry)
Parthenocissus (Boston ivy, Virginia creeper)
Picea (Spruce)
Pinus (Pine)
Rhamnus (Buckthorn)
Sambucus (Elderberry)
Smilax (Greenbrier)
Viburnum dentatum (Arrowwood)

NESTING PLANTS

Berberis (Barberry)
Cornus alternifolia, C. florida, C. mas, C. racemosa (Blue dogwood, Flowering dogwood, Cornelian cherry, Gray dogwood)
Crataegus (Hawthorn)
Elaeagnus umbellata (Autumn elaeagnus)
Fagus (Beech — trained as hedge)
Ilex (Holly — those with spiny leaves)
Juniperus virginiana (Eastern red cedar)
Lycium (Matrimony vine)
Malus (Crabapple)
Morus (Mulberry)
Picea (Spruce)
Pinus (Pine)
Rhamnus (Buckthorn)
Sambucus (Elderberry)
Tsuga (Hemlock)
Viburnum dentatum, V. lentago (Arrowwood, Nannyberry)

---

wide-angled, forking branches and if you don't clip them closely. Despite their lack of depth, other kinds of hedges offer extremely good shelter and privacy if their density is increased by periodic trimming.

START WITH A BASIC PLAN

Whether you're starting a garden from scratch or simply remodeling one already established, the first step should be to map out a carefully considered plan of action. Developing this plan will take more time than simply going to the nursery, buying small plants, and planting them. But the result will be worth it. You'll have a garden that is really pleasing—and you'll minimize disappointing results and necessary replacements.

Map your garden on paper

Begin your plan by mapping out your property on graph paper. The grid pattern will make it easy to determine distances and spacing. Then draw in the basic outlines of house, walks, patios, fences, or garages, as well as the existing plantings. Note sloping areas, soil differences, significant shade or shadow patterns, and any other physical characteristics that might influence your choice of new plants.

Don't be discouraged if your lot is small or surrounded by a heavily developed urban area. Even in an urban garden you can create a bird oasis, although certain birds will always stay closer to the outskirts of human development. A varied selection of bird-attracting plants and a variety of inviting situations (trees, massed shrubs, lawn, thicket) will go a long way toward luring the greatest potential number of bird visitors and residents.

Some "birdscaping" hints

Before you actually begin to draw up a plan for your garden, be sure to consider six basic points. Some relate specifically to plants that attract birds; others simply make good landscaping sense:

1. The gardener — not the birds — should dictate the resulting landscape. Though taking into account

the birds' requirements for food and cover, you should choose only those plants that have merit for your landscape. All garden plans should offer attractive, livable areas for both people and birds.

2. A bird's requirements are easy to satisfy without a complex design.

—Some or all of the garden's border should be thickly planted with trees and shrubs. Let large shade trees provide a canopy, smaller trees the underbrush. Selected shrubbery in between will attract ground birds.

—Keep lawn areas open, placing mass plantings of shrubs and trees around the lawn's perimeter. In large gardens with great expanses of lawn, trees with clumps of shrubs at their bases could be planted to break the grassy expanse.

—If space permits, include a grouping of dense evergreen trees for shelter.

—In the least visible part of the yard, let vines and shrubs grow wild, creating a bird "jungle."

3. In planting shrub borders, don't be monotonously even. A rectangular lawn surrounded by an unvarying 6-foot-wide shrub border may be effective — but boring.

4. Pay attention to seasonal appearances of plants before making a choice. You get the most varied effect from plants that go through some seasonal changes: spring flowers followed by colorful summer or fall fruits, or foliage that changes color in autumn.

5. Choose plants that will have mature growth in scale with your garden. An all-too-frequent mistake is the selection of plants that eventually become too large for the allotted space. A rule-of-thumb for spacing shrubs and small trees: plant them a distance apart that is ½ to ⅔ of their expected height. For quick mass effect, you can place smaller shrubs and ground cover plants closer together, later removing some of them to prevent overcrowding.

6. You may want to plant a "native garden," or at least one that will feature plants native to your part of the country. Remember that, for a garden featuring these plants, it is usually more successful to purchase them from a nursery than it is to collect the same plants in the wild. Frequently, wild plants are not easy to transplant (the mortality rate is correspondingly high) because of their widely spread root systems. A good nursery plant will have a more compact, balanced root system.

With these points clearly in mind, you're ready to plot a planting framework for an attractive garden that will attract birds. On the following pages you'll find descriptions and selected photographs of plants that attract birds in some way.

The plants are divided into functional groups: trees and shrubs (pages 53-87) and vines and ground covers (pages 89-93). Within each group plants are arranged alphabetically by their botanical names followed by their common names. Wherever more than one species

PLANT HARDINESS ZONE MAP

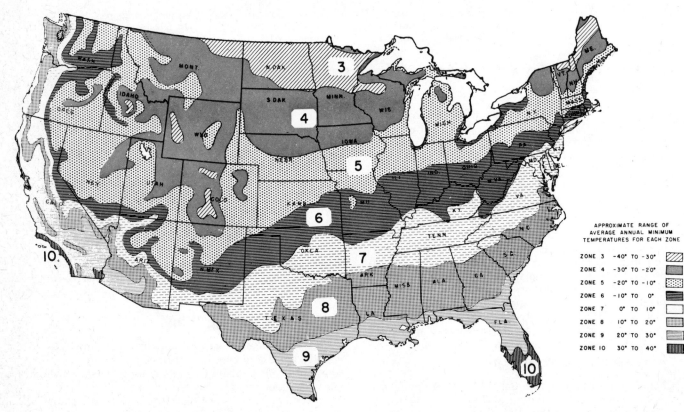

APPROXIMATE RANGE OF
AVERAGE ANNUAL MINIMUM
TEMPERATURES FOR EACH ZONE

ZONE 3   -40° TO -30°
ZONE 4   -30° TO -20°
ZONE 5   -20° TO -10°
ZONE 6   -10° TO   0°
ZONE 7   0° TO 10°
ZONE 8   10° TO 20°
ZONE 9   20° TO 30°
ZONE 10   30° TO 40°

in a particular genus is described, it is prefaced by a general description. The various species are listed in alphabetical order by their botanical names.

The zones listed with each plant represent climate adaptability conforming to the plant hardiness zone map on the opposite page. This map (compiled by the United States Department of Agriculture) is used by countless nursery catalogues and garden books to indicate where plants will grow best.

The limitations of the map are obvious. It is impossible to accurately map local variations in climate. Also, a map based only on temperatures can be misleading, because some plants also have special soil requirements. For example, blueberries and huckleberries require acid soil, but this soil will not necessarily be found throughout their range of favorable growing climates. The plant descriptions point out special cultural notes such as soil or exposure requirements not implied simply by the zoning.

Preceding each plant group is a short list of birds most likely to be attracted to the plants. In most cases the birds are interested in the food that the plant provides, but in some instances, shelter and nesting sites may also be sought. Where only one bird species is attracted to a plant, the particular species is named.

If two or more species of the same group feed on a plant, the general name is used — for example, goldfinches or grosbeaks. In a few instances it is assumed that if a bird visits a garden and feeds on the native species of a plant, it will most likely feed on a related ornamental species that is similar to the native form. Remember that birds, like most other animals, are opportunists. If the only food available is a particular berry, and the normal food of the visiting birds is fruit or berries, the bird will probably try to eat the berries.

In addition to the many woody plants that are bird favorites, birds also enjoy some annuals and perennials — and even certain weeds. The special feature on page 93 lists some of these plants and tells how they attract birds.

Without necessarily choosing any specific plants, select the plant forms you wish and sketch them onto your graph paper garden plan. Then from the descriptions, choose the specific plants best adapted to your region, your taste in landscaping, your particular garden conditions, and the birds you want to attract. Decide first where to place the largest plants — the trees. After that, work down through the tall shrubs, small shrubs, vines and ground covers, and finally, the annuals and perennials.

Trees and Shrubs

ABIES. Fir

Dense foliage provides good shelter. Network of branches offers nesting sites for robins, purple finches, grosbeaks, tanagers — even some flycatchers. In late fall, ripened cones disintegrate, scattering seeds for jays, juncos, chickadees, towhees, finches, nuthatches (including the California pigmy nuthatch). During winter months and in high elevation areas, evening and pine grosbeaks like the seeds, but yellow-bellied sapsuckers prefer the sap.

Evergreen conifers. Slow growing; dense, symmetrical, and cone or pyramid-shaped. Prefer cool, moist atmosphere and clean air; perform best across northern tier of states. In hot, dry, windy areas at low elevations, they grow slowly, if at all. Firs should not be sheared, indiscriminately pruned, or forced to fit into locations too small for them, because it ruins their regular shape and new growth often will not fill in.

A. amabilis. Silver fir. Zones 6-9. Native to coast ranges and Cascade Mountains of the Northwest; grows 20 to 50 feet tall in lowland gardens. Curving upward along branches, dark green leaves are silver underneath.

A. concolor. White fir. Zones 5-9. More adaptable than other firs to warm dry regions. Native to mountains of West where it's an important timber tree.

A. grandis. Lowland fir. Zones 6-9. Western native often found in northwest gardens. Deep green, glossy needles are 1 to 1½ inches long. Grows very tall.

A. homolepis. Nikko fir. Zones 5-9. Small fir (to 90 feet) native to Japan. Vigorous grower; has dark green needles.

A. magnifica. Red fir. Zones 6-8. Tall with blue-green needles; new growth is silvery gray. Best in Northwest and northern California.

A. nordmanniana. Nordmann fir. Zones 5-9. Modest-sized (50 feet tall, 20 feet wide) plant from southern Europe; more tolerant of heat and dryness than most other firs. Shining, dark green needles.

A. procera. Noble fir. Zones 6-9. Similar to A. magnifica but not as tall. Stiff branches of blue-green, inch-long needles.

A. spectabilis. Himalayan fir. Zones 7-9. Best fir for Southeast. Very broad pyramid, needs room to spread.

A. veitchii. Veitch fir. Zones 4-9. Hardiest of popular firs and smaller in size (to 75 feet). Needles are dark green on upper surfaces, white underneath.

ABUTILON. Flowering maple, chinese lantern

Bell-shaped flowers are hummingbird favorites. Other birds frequently come to the plants for aphids and other insects.

Evergreen vinelike shrubs. Zones 9-10. Fast growing, but tend to be loose and rangy unless new growth is periodically pinched back to promote bushiness. All have somewhat hairy, maplelike leaves, and colorful bell-shaped blossoms.

A. hybridum. Upright, arching growth 8 to 10 feet high and wide. Drooping flowers in spring are white, yellow, pink, or red. White and yellow-flowered plants may bloom over longer period. *A. striatum thompsonii* is similar plant but foliage is variegated with creamy yellow; flowers are pale orange, veined red.

A. megapotamicum. Strong growing to 10 feet high and wide. Red flowers. Leaves (to 3 inches long) are shaped like arrowheads.

A. vitifolium. Fast growth to 8 to 12 feet or more. Large leaves (to 6 inches across) and clusters of 2 to 3-inch lavender spring flowers. Best where summers are cool.

ACACIA

During the first months of spring, yellow acacia flowers (always small, fuzzy balls) offer an excellent nectar source for all types of hummingbirds. Insects in A. retinoides attract bushtits, kinglets, warblers; A. longifolia is favored by white and golden-crowned sparrows in winter.

Evergreen shrubs and trees. Extremely fast growing but relatively short-lived plants (perhaps up to 30 years). A few species definitely are shrub types, but most have the capacity to grow to tree size. If you remove the lead shoot of larger species, plant will grow as a large shrub; but stake the lead shoot and remove lower branches and you'll get a tree. Often are serviceable in "difficult" locations: hillsides, dry or poor soil, seashore plantings. A number of species may be found in nurseries; the following are some of the most popular.

A. baileyana. Bailey acacia. Tree. Zones 8-10. Good as single or multi-trunked tree to 30 feet high and wide. Feathery, finely cut blue-gray leaves. Showy clusters of yellow flowers in midwinter. Variety 'Purpurea' has lavender to purple new growth.

A. decora. Graceful wattle. Shrub. Zones 8-10. Reaches 6 to 8 feet high with equal spread, can be trimmed as hedge. Bluish, 2-inch leaves are narrow and curved. Bright clusters of yellow flower balls in spring.

A. decurrens. Green wattle. Tree. Zones 8-10. Feathery dark green leaves clothe a 50-foot tree resembling *A. baileyana* except for larger size and green color. Clus-

ters of yellow flowers come in late winter. *A. d. dealbata* is similar in all respects except that leaves, twigs, and young branches are silvery gray.

A. longifolia. Sydney golden wattle. Large shrub to 20 feet high and wide. Zones 9-10. Sometimes sold as *A. latifolia*. Bright green leaves (to 6 inches long, 2 inches wide); summer flowers bloom on short spikes along branches. Rugged plant for tough situations — along dusty roadsides, to bind soil at beach (there, wind makes plant prostrate).

A. melanoxylon. Black acacia. Upright tree to 40 feet. Zones 8-10. Poor choice for small garden or forefront planting (aggressive roots can even raise sidewalks, suckers easily, wood splits, messy leaf drop), but is fine in difficult soil and exposure situations or wherever it doesn't compete with other plants. Narrow, dark green leaves (to 4 inches long), creamy to straw colored flowers (not too conspicuous) in early spring.

A. podalyriaefolia. Pearl acacia. Shrub or small tree. Zones 9-10. May reach 20 feet high, 15 feet wide. Leaves are silvery gray and roundish (to 1½ inches long). Long clusters of fluffy light yellow flowers from late fall throughout winter.

A. retinoides. Water wattle, Floribunda acacia. Shrub (20 feet high and wide). Zones 8-10. Sometimes sold as *A. floribunda*. A not-too-dense shrub for quick screening. Narrow, yellow-green leaves are up to 5 inches long; small clusters of yellow blossoms continue to appear during most of the year in mildest areas.

A. verticillata. Star acacia. Shrub. Zones 8-10. Short, needlelike leaves in whorls give it the look of a conifer. Grown naturally, it has open growth with many trunks reaching 15 feet high and wide; can be sheared to make dense hedge. Excellent seashore plant. Pale yellow flowers in mid-spring.

Acacia baileyana *(Bailey acacia) shown here in tree form is covered with late winter flowers.*

ACER. Maple

Deciduous. Highly varied group of trees, ranging from stolid, spreading street-tree types and delicate, irregular, forest underbrush species to pyramidal forms and types suitable for hedges. Most have dense growth. Extensive, generally shallow root systems require ample water. Some of the most common species are described below.

A. campestre. Hedge maple. Zones 6-8. Useful as dense hedge or screen plant.

A. circinatum. Vine maple. Zones 6-9. Usually a multiple-trunked small tree (to 25 feet), but can be trained to a single trunk. Rounded, lobed leaves turn orange-scarlet or yellow in autumn. Graceful irregular, twisting growth if placed in shade or under taller trees; less vinelike in open locations.

A. ginnala. Amur maple. Zones 3-8. Small tree or multi-trunked large shrub. Fragrant spring flowers turn to bright red summer fruit — striking contrast to green leaves. Good red fall color.

A. negundo. Box elder. Zones 3-10. Weed tree with several points against it: seeds readily, hosts box-elder bugs, suckers badly, branches break easily. Can be useful in areas where drought and winter cold limit selection of trees. Also finds service as fast growing, temporary screen until more desirable but slower plants mature.

A. saccharum. Sugar maple. Zones 4-9. Moderate growth to 60 feet and more. Produces brilliant yellow to deep red fall color. Stout branches sweep upward to form fairly compact crown. Strictly upright forms also sold.

A. tataricum. Tatarian maple. Zones 5-9. Small tree (to about 30 feet), taller than wide. Red fruit in summer is followed by yellow to red autumn colors.

AESCULUS

Deciduous tree and large shrub. Large, somewhat coarse, tropical appearing leaves are divided fanwise into large leaflets. Flowers are in long, dense, showy clusters at ends of branches. No autumn color.

A. californica. California buckeye. Zones 7-9. A wide-spreading shrub or small tree (often with several trunks) to about 20 feet high, sometimes wider. Creamy flower spikes appear in mid-spring. Rich green leaves (leaflets to 6 inches long) turn brown and drop by mid-summer unless plants receive regular watering. Bare trunk and branches are attractive silvery gray.

A. carnea. Red horsechestnut. Zones 5-9. Dense, round-headed tree to 50 feet high, somewhat less wide. Spikes of soft pink to red flowers in mid-spring (A. c. 'Briotii' has rosy crimson blooms). Leaflets may be up to 10 inches long.

ALBIZIA

Deciduous to semi-evergreen trees. Finely divided, fernlike foliage and clusters of fluffy flowers give these trees a tropical mimosalike appearance.

A. distachya. Plume albizia. Semi-evergreen. Zones 9-10. Sometimes sold as A. lophantha. Fast growing to 20 feet, with dark velvety green foliage. Late spring flowers are greenish yellow. Grows well in poor soils (even pure beach sand) but is fairly short lived.

A. julibrissin. Silk tree. Deciduous. Zones 7-10. Fast growth to 40 feet with wider spread. Form is flat-topped, often branching very low (unless trained early), or multiple trunked. Foliage is light green; leaflets fold up at night. Fluffy pink flowers look like pincushions; variety 'Rosea' has darker pink flowers and is hardy into Zone 6.

ALNUS. Alder

Deciduous trees. Valuable for rapid growth and preference for moist or wet soils. Upright growth taller than wide. Tent caterpillars can disfigure tree.

A. cordata. Italian alder. Zones 6-10. Grows to 40 feet. Glossy, rich green leaves are heart shaped and about 4 inches long.

(Continued on next page)

Alnus cordata (Italian alder) *has hanging seed clusters in winter; several bird species eat them.*

...Alnus (cont'd.)

A. incana. Speckled alder. Zones 3-8. Dark green leaves have no autumn color. Especially cold tolerant.

A. oregona. Red alder. Zones 7-9. Unusually tolerant of brackish water. Grows to 50 feet.

A. rhombifolia. White alder. Zones 6-9. Gray-white bark good contrast to dark green foliage. Growing wild, may reach 90 feet; is somewhat shorter in cultivation.

AMELANCHIER. Service berry

Good choice for berry eaters. Favoring the A. alnifolia are black-headed and evening grosbeaks, western tanagers, northern orioles, western bluebirds, rufous-sided towhees, robins, chestnut-backed chickadees, mockingbirds, house finches. Preferring the A. canadensis are cedar waxwings; common flickers; blue jays; downy, hairy, and red-headed woodpeckers; hermit and Swainson's thrushes. Phoebes, eastern bluebirds, mourning doves, kingbirds, rose-breasted grosbeaks, brown thrashers, red-eyed vireos, song sparrows, robins, scarlet tanagers are partial to A. laevis. Catbirds favor A. stolonifera.

Deciduous shrubs or small trees. Attractive in all seasons. Very showy clusters of white flowers appear in early spring before leaves; small edible fruits in summer. Have colorful autumn foliage, attractive winter branch and twig pattern. Roots are not invasive, shade is not heavy.

A. alnifolia. Western or Saskatoon service berry. Zones 4-8. Tall shrub, 12 to 15 feet. Small 1 to 2-inch-long leaves open bronzy red, change to dark and then pale green in summer, and finally to yellow and dusty red in autumn. Tiny blue-black fruits come in summer.

A. canadensis. Shadblow service berry. Zones 5-8. Slender tree to 30 feet or more; sometimes shrubby. New leaves are pinkish gray, turn yellow to red in fall; fruit is dark red.

A. grandiflora. Apple service berry. Zones 5-8. Spreading growth builds up to 25 feet; light gray bark. Largest flowers of all service berries; a little over an inch across. Fruit is red to black while fall color is in yellow-orange range.

A. laevis. Shadbush, Allegany service berry. Zones 5-8. Thirty-five-foot tree with attractive gray bark. New foliage is purplish and flowers come in long, drooping clusters. Fruit is red; fall color is yellow to red.

A. stolonifera. Creeping service berry. Zones 5-8. Grows about 4 feet tall; spreads by underground roots (stolons) to form thickets. Grows well in poor, dry soil; good for holding soil that might erode.

ARBUTUS

Spring flowers eaten by black-headed grosbeaks. Ripening berries enjoyed by robins, Steller's jays, Townsend's solitaires, cedar waxwings, mockingbirds, acorn woodpeckers, varied thrushes. Berries falling to the ground provide food for California quail, towhees, song and white-crowned sparrows, flickers, grosbeaks.

Evergreen tree and shrub-tree. Both have bark that peels off to reveal red-brown trunk and limbs. Western native rarely succeeds outside native range.

A. menziesii. Madrone, Madrona. Zones 7-9. Large shrub or tree ranging from 25 to 100 feet. Native from British Columbia into California. Handsome, leathery leaves are rhododendronlike. White, bell-shaped blossoms are similar to those of manzanitas and heathers. Leaves are followed by orange to red berries. Smooth reddish-brown bark continually peels off in thin flakes. Plants must have acid to neutral soil and water, excellent drainage, and infrequent but deep watering. Constant drop of leaves, bark, or fruit may be nuisance in some landscape situations.

A. unedo. Strawberry tree. Shrub-tree. Zones 8-10. Slow to moderate growth; may reach 35 feet, but growth habit is shrubby unless trained to single trunk. Oblong dark green leaves are 2 to 3 inches long; trunk and branches have red-brown, shreddy bark. Clusters of small, white, urn-shaped flowers appear in fall and winter; are immediately followed by red and yellow,

Arbutus unedo *(Strawberry tree) has strawberry-colored fruits when ripe; texture is rough, prickly.*

¾-inch round fruit. Quite adaptable to soils and climates within its range; in hottest regions, plant in shade.

ARCTOSTAPHYLOS. Manzanita

Eating insects, spring flowers, or fruits are towhees, fox sparrows, grosbeaks, jays, thrashers, varied thrushes, mockingbirds, California quail, wrentits, acorn woodpeckers.

Evergreen shrubs. Waxy, bell-like flowers and fruits resembling tiny apples characterize manzanitas. Many have attractive crooked branches and smooth red to purple bark. Best in loose and well-drained soil; in other soils the safest location is on a bank or slope. Wild manzanitas grow without summer water; garden manzanitas require weekly watering during the first year, about once a month in following summers (even less if soil is not too well drained). Flowers usually appear in late winter and early spring. Many species and varieties spread widely and grow up to about 2 feet high, so are better considered as ground covers. The following are definitely shrubby.

A. columbiana. Hairy manzanita. Zones 7-9. Open, strongly branched shrub growing from 3 to 15 feet tall. Bark is red-brown to red-purple; branches have long white hairs, while 3-inch, oval, gray-green leaves also sport white fur.

A. densiflora 'Sentinel'. Zones 8-9. Distinctly upright growth to 6 or more feet with spread to about 8 feet. Leaves are light green and downy; smooth bark is reddish black.

A. insularis. Island manzanita. Zones 9-10. Eight-foot-high shrub of spreading rather than upright habit.

Bright green, oval leaves to 2 inches long are set off against dark red bark. Tolerates moderate summer watering — more so than most manzanitas.

A. manzanita. Common manzanita. Zones 7-10. Large (6 to 30 feet tall), often picturesquely twisted shrub; growth is basically upright, never wider than tall. Flowers turn from white to pink; fruit begins white but ripens to deep red.

A. stanfordiana 'Louis Edmunds'. Zones 7-9. Upright growth 5 to 6 feet, with red-brown bark and glossy deep green foliage. Pink flowers are followed by red to red-brown fruits.

ARONIA. Chokeberry

Good choice for fruit eaters. Red and purple chokeberries attract cedar waxwings, bluebirds, gray catbirds, brown thrashers. A. melanocarpa is favored by brown thrashers, gray catbirds, bobwhites, and some 20 other bird species.

Deciduous shrubs. Chokeberries are noted for their easy culture, good fall foliage color, and attractive fruits that persist after leaves drop. Spring display of white flowers is attractive, if not dramatically showy.

A. arbutifolia. Red chokeberry. Zones 5-8. Large, openly branched, upright shrub; grows 6 to 10 feet high. Narrow, oval leaves are about 3 inches long, dark green above but gray and feltlike beneath. Abundant, brilliant red, ¼-inch fruits ripen as foliage turns red in early autumn. Native to swamplands but will easily grow in normal (or less than normal) garden moisture.

A. atropurpurea. Purple chokeberry. Zones 5-8. Taller than *A. arbutifolia* (to 12 feet). Bears purple-black fruits.

A. melanocarpa. Black chokeberry. Zones 5-8. Shorter shrub, usually to around 3 feet. Has narrower, shiny leaves. Autumn leaf color is purplish red, while berries are black. Native to fairly dry situations so is the best adapted of chokeberries to dry garden soils.

ATRIPLEX. Saltbush

Several species of sparrows, towhees, finches, doves, quail (and occasionally thrashers) may feed on seeds.

Evergreen or deciduous shrubs. Unusually tolerant of direct seashore conditions or highly alkaline desert soils. Add gray or silvery foliage to a landscape.

A. canescens. Four-wing saltbush. Evergreen. Zones 6-10. Dense growth to 6 feet high, 8 feet wide, with narrow gray leaves. Good for hedges, either clipped or unclipped.

(Continued on next page)

A. halimus. Mediterranean saltbush. Semi-evergreen. Zones 8-10. Dense plant to 6 feet high and wide with roundish, silvery leaves. Good for clipped or unclipped hedges.

A. hymenelytra. Desert holly. Evergreen. Zones 6-10. Compact 1 to 3-foot shrub with whitish branches and silvery, hollylike leaves. In areas where it doesn't grow wild it must have excellently drained soil and no summer water unless drainage is fast.

A. lentiformis. Quail bush. Deciduous. Zones 8-9. Densely branched and often spiny, to 10 feet tall and 12 feet wide. Oval, bluish-gray leaves to 2 inches long. Good hedge or windbreak. Salt tolerant.

A. l. breweri. Brewer saltbush. Nearly evergreen. Zones 9-10. Plant is like the preceding species without spines. Good along seacoast. Another that can be used as hedge.

BELOPERONE. SHRIMP PLANT

Throughout long blooming season, shrimp-shaped flower clusters offer nectar to hummingbirds. Mockingbirds and white-crowned sparrows eat parts of flowers.

Evergreen shrub. Zones 9-10. Left alone, a rather sprawling, mound-shaped plant to 4 feet high and wide. Egg-shaped leaves (to 2½ inches long) are apple green. Drooping flower spike (from which tubular white blossoms emerge) is 3 to 6 inches long and composed of coppery bronze overlapping bracts, giving the shrimp appearance. The variety 'Chartreuse' has yellow-green bracts. Needs frequent pinching of new growth to prevent sprawling growth. Good container plant.

BERBERIS. BARBERRY

Mainly used for cover. Mockingbirds, cedar waxwings, robins, dark-eyed juncos, gray catbirds, thrushes, rose-breasted grosbeaks eat berries only when other food is scarce.

Deciduous and evergreen shrubs. Barberries are noted for the climate and soil extremes they can withstand. Requiring, at most, no more than ordinary garden care, all are vigorous, thorny shrubs ideally suited for use as impenetrable hedge or barrier plantings. Most make handsome specimen shrubs, offering yellow flowers, colorful autumn foliage, and attractive small berries. Some species are alternate hosts for a disease that affects cereal crops, but all recommended below are classified as disease resistant and should be safe to plant even in grain producing regions.

B. buxifolia. Magellan barberry. Evergreen. Zones 6-9. Rather rigid upright growth to 6 feet high and wide. Small, leathery leaves are up to 1 inch long. Orange-yellow flowers are followed by dark purple berries. Variety 'Nana' grows to 1½ feet high and 2 feet wide.

B. darwinii. Darwin barberry. Evergreen. Zones 8-9. Fountainlike growth reaches 5 to 10 feet high with 4 to 7-foot spread. One-inch leaves are dark green and hollylike. Orange-yellow flowers are so thick along branches that foliage is nearly obscured; berries are dark blue. Plants spread by underground runners.

B. gagnepainii. Black barberry. Evergreen. Zones 6-9. Open, rangy growth will reach 6 feet high. Narrow dark green leaves are up to 3 inches long with spiny edges. Black berries have blue-gray cast.

B. julianae. Wintergreen barberry. Evergreen to semi-deciduous. Zones 6-9. Dense, upright shrub to 6 feet. Very leathery, dark green leaves (up to 3 inches long) have spiny margins, grow on especially thorny branches. Fruits are bluish black.

B. koreana. Korean barberry. Deciduous. Zones 6-9. Growth is upright and arching, becoming more spreading in age. Pendant clusters of bright yellow flowers appear with fresh green spring leaves; flowers become bright red berries that persist into winter. Autumn foliage color is deep red.

B. mentorensis. Mentor barberry. Semi-deciduous. Zones 6-9. A hybrid between *B. julianae* and *B. thunbergii*. Most cold tolerant of barberries that tend to remain evergreen. Also is able to withstand hot, dry summers better than other species. Growth is compact and upright to 7 feet high and wide. Dark green, spiny 1-inch leaves; berries are dull, dark red.

B. stenophylla. Rosemary barberry. Evergreen to deciduous, depending on severity of winter. Zones 6-9. Slender, arching branches grow 3 to 9 feet high (on the short side where winters are coldest). Narrow, inch-long leaves are dark green on top, paler below. Nodding flower clusters followed by black fruits.

B. thunbergii. Japanese barberry. Deciduous. Zones 5-9. Especially rugged; tolerates nearly any soil, dry conditions, and shade. Graceful growth habit: slender, arching branches reach 4 to 6 feet high and as wide, densely foliaged with rounded, ½ to 1½-inch deep green leaves. Leaves turn yellow, orange, and red before they fall. Beadlike bright red berries hang on throughout winter. Variety 'Atropurpurea' has bronzy red to purple-red foliage throughout spring and summer but needs full sun to develop color.

B. triacanthophora. Three-spine barberry. Evergreen. Zones 7-9. Perhaps most cold tolerant of completely evergreen barberries; grows to 5 feet high and wide. Narrow, 1 to 2-inch leaves are spiny-edged, dark green above but grayish beneath. Flowers are white tinged with red, and are followed by blue-black berries.

B. verruculosa. Warty barberry. Evergreen. Zones 7-9. Neat, tailored shrub that will reach 3 to 4 feet high but can easily be kept to half that height. Glossy dark green leaves have white undersides, turn bronze in autumn or remain green with scattered red leaves.

BETULA. BIRCH

Various birds like seeds and buds. Dark-eyed juncos, bluejays, tufted titmice like the B. lenta. Drawn to other birch species are purple finches, towhees, goldfinches, pine siskins, cedar waxwings, bobwhites. Warblers, chickadees, vireos, bushtits, northern orioles, and other insect eaters search for aphids, leaf miners, measuring worms, and other insects.

Deciduous trees. Although some birches grow quite tall, they are never massive, always graceful. Foliage turns yellow in autumn.

B. lenta. Sweet birch. Zones 4-8. Red-brown to blackish bark looks more like that of a cherry tree than a birch. Grows to 75 feet, is round headed at maturity. Young trees are pyramid shaped.

B. lutea. Yellow birch. Zones 4-8. Native to moist woodlands from extreme Northeast states to Georgia. Grows to 75 feet; has leaves up to 5 inches long. Flaky bark is yellowish to silver.

B. nigra. River birch. Zones 5-10. Very fast, pyramidal growth 50 to 90 feet. Young bark is pinkish, very smooth and shining; on older trees it flakes and curls in cinnamon brown to blackish sheets. Diamond-shaped leaves (1 to 3 inches) are glossy green on top, silvery underneath. Needs ample water; can tolerate standing in water for periods of a few weeks.

B. papyrifera. Canoe birch. Zones 3-8. Similar to *B. verrucosa*, but more open and less weeping, with larger (to 4 inches long) and fewer leaves. Trunks are creamy white; bark peels off in paper layers.

B. populifolia. Gray birch. Zones 5-8. Bark is white with numerous black markings. Tends to grow (up to 30 feet) in multi-trunked clumps. Tolerates variety of soils, from poor and rocky to quite wet.

B. verrucosa. European white birch. Zones 3-10. Reaches 30 to 50 feet, spreads about half as wide. Delicate and lacy, main branches grow upright but side branches weep. Bark on trunk and main limbs is white, marked with black clefts, but is golden brown on twigs and young branches. Usual shape is pyramidal, but selected forms are strongly weeping, bolt upright, or with finely dissected leaves.

BROUSSONETIA papyrifera. PAPER MULBERRY

Fruits eaten by cardinals, robins, gray catbirds, mockingbirds, brown thrashers.

Deciduous tree. Zones 6-10. Useful as shade tree in difficult locations. Takes alkaline soil, strong wind, smoke, dust, and desert heat. Moderate growth to 50 feet with dense crown nearly as wide. Heart-shaped leaves (4 to 8 inches long) are irregularly lobed; texture is rough and hairy. Trunk is gray. Small fruit in summer is orange to red. Suckers freely in good soils or if roots are disturbed.

BUDDLEIA davidii. COMMON BUTTERFLY BUSH

Hummingbirds favor summer flowers. Flower nectar also attracts insects which bring insect-eating birds.

Deciduous to semi-evergreen shrub. Zones 6-10. Fast, vigorous growth to 10 to 15 feet. Dark green, tapered leaves are 4 to 12 inches long, undersides are felted white. In summer plant bears slender clusters (to a foot or more long) of lilac-colored flowers with orange centers. Many named varieties are sold with different flower colors: white, pink, dark red, purple, and blue to lilac. Only needs well-drained soil and regular watering for good growth. Freezes to the ground in coldest areas within its hardiness range, but comes back mightily from the roots in spring. Severe annual cutting back often necessary to prevent plant from becoming ratty.

CALLICARPA. BEAUTY BERRY

Fruit attracts mockingbirds, robins, brown thrashers, cardinals, red-eyed towhees, hermit thrushes, gray catbirds, bobwhites.

Deciduous shrubs. Flowers are inconspicuous, but fruit is decorative feature. Freeze to ground in severe win-

Callicarpa japonica *(Japanese beauty berry) bears small berries of an eye-catching violet color.*

ters but will resprout from roots. Because blooms and berries are borne on new wood, annual pruning or freezing is not detrimental.

C. bodinieri giraldii. Zones 6-8. Six to 10-foot plant with gracefully recurving branches. Narrow, 4-inch leaves resemble those of peaches; turn pink or purple in autumn. Flowers are lilac colored, followed by violet-purple, pea-sized berries.

C. dichotoma. Korean beauty berry. Zones 6-8. Upright growth reaches 6 feet, clothed in oval, 3-inch leaves. Both foliage and stems turn purplish in fall. Tiny pink spring flowers; pinkish violet fruits in autumn.

C. japonica. Japanese beauty berry. Zones 6-8. Five-foot, upright shrub. Leaves turn light yellow in autumn; against these are displayed violet-colored berries.

CALLISTEMON. BOTTLEBRUSH

Hummingbirds are drawn to flower nectar. Orioles also feed on nectar and on insects that flowers attract. Tanagers and migrating warblers eat insects.

Evergreen shrubs (a few can be treelike). Zones 9-10. The bottlebrush look comes from dense flower clusters or spikes that consist principally of long, threadlike stamens. Fast growing. Tolerate drought and alkaline soils, but grow best in moist, well-drained soil. For similar "bottlebrushes," see *Melaleuca* (page 74). A number of species and varieties are sold; these are among the most widespread.

C. citrinus. Lemon bottlebrush. Large shrub to 15 feet, or small tree (with training) to 25 feet. Narrow leaves (to 3 inches long) are copper colored when new, change to bright green. Brilliant red brushes (to 6 inches long) appear periodically throughout the year.

C. linearis. Narrow-leafed bottlebrush. Loose, airy growth to 8 feet tall, 5 feet wide, with narrow, 5-inch leaves that turn purplish as they mature. Bright crimson, 5-inch brushes in summer. Variety 'Pumila' is shorter form (to 6 feet).

C. phoeniceus. Fiery bottlebrush. A 6 to 8-foot shrub similar to *C. citrinus* but is stiffer and more densely foliaged, with light green to gray leaves. Variety 'Prostrata' is a sprawling version (to 6 feet).

C. rigidus. Stiff bottlebrush. Erect, rigid, and sparse shrub to 20 feet high, 10 feet wide. Leaves sharp-pointed, gray-green. Red flower brushes in clusters to 4½ inches long, spring and summer. The most drought-tolerant species.

C. viminalis. Weeping bottlebrush. Shrub or small tree with drooping branches. Fast to 20 to 30 feet with 15-foot spread. Narrow, light green, 6-inch leaves. Biggest show of bright red brushes is mid-spring to midsummer, but scattered blooms appear all year. Needs ample water. Often looks sparse, as leaves tend to grow only at ends of long, hanging branches. Variety 'Mc-Caskillii' is more dense.

CARISSA grandiflora. NATAL PLUM

Robins, mockingbirds, house finches eat fruit.

Evergreen shrub. Zones 9-10. Neat, polished, fast growing to 5 to 7 feet. Has plenty of spines to discourage both people and animals. Lustrous, leathery, deep green leaves are 3-inch ovals; fragrant, white, star-shaped flowers reach 2 inches across. One to 2-inch red, plum-shaped fruits are edible. Easy to grow within its hardiness limit; takes variety of soils and exposures, including ocean wind and salt spray. Can be pruned to make formal hedge. Numerous named varieties are sold, most of which are lower growing and more wide spreading.

CARPINUS caroliniana. AMERICAN HORNBEAM

Good nesting sites. Small, nutlike fruits eaten by cardinals, American goldfinches, evening grosbeaks, bobwhites.

Deciduous tree. Zones 3-9. Moderate growth to round headed, 25 to 30 feet. Leaves are dark green (1 to 3 inches long) with toothed edges, and turn yellow to red in fall. Bark is gray.

CEANOTHUS. WILD LILAC

Attracts number of visiting birds, many eating insects on ground beneath plants: quail, wrentits, bushtits, grosbeaks, sparrows, towhees, thrashers, dark-eyed juncos. In southwestern regions attracts finches, mockingbirds, thrushes, white-crowned sparrows. Blossoms attract hummingbirds and, occasionally, warblers and flycatchers.

Evergreen shrubs or small trees. Upright to spreading shrubs (depending on variety or species) with small, glossy, and somewhat wrinkled leaves. Clusters of tiny flowers in white or all shades of blue give a lilac appearance. Many are highly intolerant of regular watering during summer and will quickly die from root rot. A smaller number tolerate some summer water or even regular watering. All should be planted in well-drained soil.

C. arboreus. Feltleaf ceanothus. Zones 8-10. Large shrub or small tree to 25 feet, with oval leaves (2 to 3 inches long) and pale blue flowers. Good garden tolerance. Variety 'Ray Hartman' has blue flowers.

C. 'Concha'. Zones 8-10. Shrub to 6 feet, with small clusters of dark blue flowers. Good garden tolerance.

C. cyaneus 'Sierra Blue'. Shrub. Zones 7-10. To 12 feet high with masses of deep blue flowers. Good garden tolerance.

C. griseus 'Louis Edmunds'. Shrub. Zones 8-10. Grows 4 to 5 feet high, up to 12 feet wide. Small clusters of violet-blue flowers. Good garden tolerance. Variety 'Santa Ana' spreads to 20 feet, has pure blue blossoms, excellent garden tolerance.

C. impressus 'Mountain Haze'. Shrub. Zones 7-10. Grows to 4 feet with little water, to 12 feet under normal garden watering. Dense plant with bright blue flowers. Excellent garden tolerance.

C. 'Julia Phelps'. Shrub. Zones 8-10. Rounded, dense plant to 8 feet high and wide. Striking deep blue flowers in small clusters; fairly good garden tolerance.

C. rigidus 'Snowball'. Shrub. Zones 8-10. Distinct, rounded white flower clusters grow along rigid, open, spreading branches. Grows to 4 to 5 feet high, with fair garden tolerance.

C. velutinus. Tobacco brush. Shrub. Zones 5-8. Rounded plant, 2 to 5 feet high. Dark green leaves have varnished look on upper surface, are velvety gray beneath. Creamy white flowers appear in dense clusters in late spring through summer. Good garden tolerance.

CELTIS. HACKBERRY

Popular food tree for berry eaters. C. douglasii commonly visited by Townsend's solitaires, evening grosbeaks, robins, hermit thrushes. C. laevigata and C. occidentalis are liked by eastern bluebirds, cardinals, common flickers, mockingbirds, robins, brown thrashers, phoebes, yellow-bellied sapsuckers, bobwhites, cedar waxwings, hermit thrushes. Desert area hackberries attract finches, Gambel's quail, Bendire's and curve-billed thrashers; white-winged doves which also find excellent nesting sites in the hackberry in spring.

Deciduous trees. Related and similar to elms in many respects, but smaller. Deep rooted. When established, take desert heat, wind, drought, and alkaline soil.

C. australis. European hackberry. Zones 7-9. Can reach 40 feet in 15 years, ultimately to about 75 feet. In contrast to *C. occidentalis* is more upright and never as wide spreading, with longer (to 5 inches), more pointed leaves, and shorter deciduous period.

C. douglasii. Western hackberry. Zones 4-8. Reaches 25 to 30 feet with similar spread; branches are somewhat pendulous. Oval leaves are 4 inches long.

C. laevigata. Sugarberry, Mississippi hackberry. Zones 6-8. Grows to 100 feet in native eastern states, but is about half that height elsewhere. Develops spreading, round-headed, open crown with somewhat pendulous branches. Resistant to witches' broom disease.

C. occidentalis. Common hackberry. Zones 3-10. Native to eastern states; particularly susceptible to disfiguring witches' broom disease in that area. In other regions this disease is not bothersome. Quite late to leaf out in spring.

CERCIDIUM. PALO VERDE

Blossoms attract hummingbirds, cactus wrens. Desert region species visited by finches, mockingbirds. Seeds eaten by doves, sparrows, bobwhites, quail.

Deciduous trees. Zones 8-9. Two species are native to southwest deserts: *C. floridum* and *C. microphyllum*. Plants are similar except for color of leaves and bark — bluish green in the first species, yellow-green in the second. Fast growing to 25 feet high and wide. In spring, 2 to 4½-inch-long clusters of small yellow flowers almost hide branches. Out of bloom, plants are intricate pattern of spiny branches, branchlets, and leaf stalks. Drought resistant, but are more dense, attractive, and faster growing with additional water and some fertilizer.

CESTRUM nocturnum. NIGHT JESSAMINE

Favored by hummingbirds; warblers pierce night-blooming flowers to drink nectar. White berries are relished by mockingbirds and many other berry-eating birds.

Evergreen shrub. Zones 8-10. Fast growing and rather rangy, with light green, long (4 to 8 inches), lance-shaped leaves. Clusters of powerfully fragrant (at night) creamy white flowers in summer are followed by white berries.

CHAENOMELES. FLOWERING QUINCE

Winter blooms on red-flowering forms are special hummingbird favorites.

Deciduous shrubs. Zones 5-9. Among the earliest shrubs to flower — often beginning in midwinter in the milder zones. Many named hybrids are sold, varying in color of flowers (white, shades of pink, brilliant to dark red) and growth habit (some grow to 10 feet high and spreading wider; some are compact and low growing). Most are thorny. General characteristics are: shiny green leaves (to 2 inches long) with tinges of red when young, angular branching habit that forms dense plants. All are easy to grow, tolerate light to heavy soil (but may become chlorotic in alkaline soils). Prune or thin out plants at any time to shape.

CHILOPSIS linearis. DESERT WILLOW

Spring (and sometimes fall) lobed-shaped flowers attract hummingbirds.

Deciduous large shrub or small tree. Zones 7-9. Open, airy plant with long (to 6 inches), narrow, willowlike leaves. Can be trained as a tree to about 25 feet high. Fast growing when young. Tubular flowers in spring may be pink, rose, white, or lavender marked with purple; nurseries may sell selected color forms. Old plants develop shaggy bark and picturesque, twisting trunks. Garden plants are much better looking than those growing wild. Drops leaves early unless it is watered regularly.

CHIONANTHUS virginicus. FRINGE TREE

Dark blue fruits eaten by some woodpeckers but not liked by many other bird species.

Deciduous tree. Zones 5-9. May reach 30 feet in native eastern seaboard regions, but is apt to be slow growing and shrubby elsewhere. Lacy clusters of white flowers in spring are followed by clusters of dark blue, grape-like fruits. Broad, oval leaves turn bright yellow in autumn. Very late to leaf out in spring.

CORNUS. DOGWOOD

Fruit-bearing tree with good nesting sites. More than 90 bird species like the berries, particularly eastern bluebirds, gray catbirds, common flickers, robins, black-headed and rose-breasted grosbeaks, mockingbirds, cardinals, summer tanagers, sparrows, brown thrashers, cedar waxwings, woodpeckers (including the hairy, downy, red-headed, and red-bellied species), purple finches, Swainson's thrushes, red-eyed vireos, bobwhites. Insect eaters particularly like the C. stolonifera which has a long flowering and fruit season. Favoring the C. capitata are scrub and Steller's jays, white and golden-crowned sparrows, thrushes, titmice. Insect eaters include tanagers and warblers.

Deciduous (except where noted) shrubs or trees. Dogwood "flowers" are leafy bracts surrounding inconspicuous real flowers which produce fruit. Shrub species are generally less spectacular in flower than flowering tree species, but do provide good fall color and winter interest, often with colorful branches and fruits. Quite easy to grow and trouble free; all require moist soil.

C. alba. Tatarian dogwood. Shrub. Zones 3-10. Upright to about 10 feet and wide spreading. Eventually produces many-stemmed thicket. Branches are densely clothed with 2½ to 5-inch-long, oval leaves that are dark green becoming red in fall. Clusters of small, fragrant, creamy white flowers appear in spring, forming white or bluish white berries in fall. Branches and twigs are bright red, especially attractive in winter against a background of snow.

C. a. 'Sibirica'. Siberian dogwood. Less rampant than the species, grows to about 7 feet high and 5 feet wide. Branches are coral red in winter.

C. alternifolia. Blue dogwood. Zones 4-9. Shrubby to 15 feet, but can also be trained as small tree. Oval leaves are 2 to 4 inches long. Small clusters of white flowers produce dark blue autumn fruits.

C. amomum. Silky dogwood. Shrub. Zones 6-9. Native of eastern states. Quite similar to C. a. 'Sibirica' but later flowering and has less brilliant red twigs. Berries appear in varying shades of blue.

C. capitata. Evergreen dogwood. Big shrub or small tree. Zones 8-9. In coldest areas of its adaptability it may not remain evergreen or may retain only part of its leaves. Moderate growth to 20 to 40 feet, eventually as wide; may grow into large shrub unless trained as tree. Leathery green to gray-green leaves measure up to 4 inches long and 2 inches wide, some turning red or purplish in fall. Flower bracts are cream or pale yellow.

C. controversa. Giant dogwood. Tree. Zones 6-9. Tiered branch structure is strongly horizontal. Grows rapidly to mature height of 40 to 60 feet. Oval leaves (3 to 6 inches long) are dark green on top, silvery green underneath. White "flowers" are small but very profuse. Red autumn foliage.

C. florida. Flowering dogwood. Tree. Zones 5-9. Matures into 20 to 40-foot tree with horizontal branching pattern. White flower bracts form "flowers" (2 to 4 inches across), nearly covering tree before spring leaf-out. Numerous named varieties, with flower bracts in varying shades of pink to nearly red, can be purchased. Oval leaves (2 to 6 inches long) turn to glowing red in autumn. Fruit also is red.

C. kousa. Kousa, Japanese dogwood. Big shrub or small tree. Zones 6-9. Similar in some respects to C. florida but blooms about one month later after leafing out. Branching pattern is horizontal, but without training tends to grow as shorter (20 to 25 feet), large, multistemmed shrub. Flower bracts are white with pointed tips. In autumn red fruits hang below branches like big strawberries.

C. mas. Cornelian cherry. Shrub or tree. Zones 5-8. By natural inclination an airy, twiggy shrub. Can be trained as 15 to 25-foot rounded, dense tree. Shiny green oval leaves (2 to 4 inches long) turn yellow (occasionally red) in autumn. Bright scarlet fruits enhance fall color display. Tolerates alkaline soils.

C. racemosa. Gray dogwood. Shrub. Zones 5-9. Growth is upright and dense to 15 feet; can stand shearing and cutting to serve as hedge. In summer white fruits

Cornus florida (Dogwood) left, has showy bracts surrounding tiny flowers. **Upper right:** C. stolonifera (Redtwig dogwood) berries are typical of dogwood fruit. **Lower right:** C. mas (Cornelian cherry) has larger fruit.

ripen on red stalks; remain even after leaves fall. Narrow, 4-inch leaves turn purplish in autumn; winter branches are gray.

C. sanguinea. Bloodtwig dogwood. Shrub. Zones 5-8. Grows as big, upright clump to 12 feet high and 8 feet wide. Dark green, oval, 3-inch leaves turn to dark blood red in autumn; after leaves fall, black fruits decorate red branches.

C. stolonifera. Red-osier, Redtwig dogwood. Shrub. Zones 3-9. Because it tends to spread widely by creeping underground stems and rooting branches, this species is best in naturalistic plantings or where it has plenty of room. Growth is rapid, to 10 to 15 feet high. Prefers moist soil although it will get by with less than normal garden watering. White or blue-white fruits ripen in summer. Autumn foliage color is red, followed by equally brilliant pattern of red branches.

COTONEASTER

Excellent shrub for fruit eaters. Visitors may include bluebirds, robins, cedar waxwings, mockingbirds, house finches, thrushes. Hummingbirds like spring flowers.

Evergreen and deciduous. Some are huge, arching shrubs or shrub-trees, others are just bushy, and some are low ground covers (see page 90). Most cotoneasters have similar characteristics — fairly small, oval leaves; flattish clusters of small white flowers; small, red, applelike fruit. All grow vigorously and thrive with little or no maintenance, preferring well-drained, average soil.

With so many species and varieties available — and offerings varying from one part of the country to another — it's best to ask your local nurseryman to help you select a cotoneaster. The prominent berries of one species, C. parneyi, are not eaten by birds.

CRATAEGUS. Hawthorn

Forty bird species eat the fruit. Resembling miniature apples, the seedy fruit is particularly enjoyed by cedar waxwings (and the rare Bohemian waxwing in northwestern regions), grosbeaks (evening, pine, and blackheaded), blue jays, mockingbirds, robins, fox sparrows, hermit thrushes, purple finches, quail, common flickers. Feeding on aphids and caterpillars that usually attack this tree may be bushtits, chickadees, several species of warblers. Good nesting sites for hummingbirds.

Deciduous trees. Noted for attractive spring flowers (white, unless noted otherwise) and showy fruits in summer, fall, or winter. If attractive wild hawthorns grow in your area, consider planting them in your garden rather than exotic species or varieties. Nearly all are dense with thorny branches; need some pruning to thin out excess, twiggy growth. Fireblight may cause entire branches to die back quickly. If this happens, cut out blighted branches well below dead part and wash pruning tool with disinfectant between each cut. Keep plants on dry side to avoid rank, succulent growth which is particularly susceptible to fireblight.

C. arnoldiana. Arnold hawthorn. Zones 5-9. Thirty-foot, round-headed tree. Bears earliest fruits of all hawthorns, often ripening in mid-August.

C. crus-galli. Cockspur thorn. Zones 5-9. Round-headed tree to 35 feet (or huge shrub, without training), with distinctive horizontal branching pattern. Following an orange to red fall foliage display, bright red fruit hangs on during winter.

C. lavallei. Carriere or Lavalle hawthorn. Zones 5-9. More erect and open branching with less twiggy growth than other hawthorns. Mature trees may be 25 feet tall, spreading only 10 feet. Handsome, leathery dark green leaves are 2 to 4 inches long; turn bronze-red after first sharp frost and hang on into winter. Loose clusters of ¾-inch, red-orange fruits also persist through winter.

C. oxyacantha. English hawthorn. Zones 5-9. Moderate growth to 18 to 25 feet with nearly equal spread. Leaves are 2 inches long with 3 to 7-inch lobes, but without distinctive fall color. Fruits ripening in fall are about 1 inch in diameter. Number of selected forms and named varieties are sold, some with pink to nearly red flowers and some with double blossoms which bear few fruits.

C. phaenopyrum. Washington thorn. Zones 5-9. More graceful and delicate than most other hawthorns; much better street or lawn tree. Of hawthorns, it is the least susceptible to fireblight. Growth is broadly upright to 30 feet with about a 20-foot spread. Glossy leaves are 2 to 3 inches long and somewhat maplelike with three to five sharply pointed lobes; turn bright orange to red in autumn. Shiny red fruits in fall hang on well into winter.

ELAEAGNUS

Cherrylike fruit of *E. multiflora* eaten by eastern bluebirds, cardinals, gray catbirds, pine grosbeaks, ruby-throated hummingbirds (primarily interested in flowers), blue jays, thrushes, cedar waxwings, robins, mockingbirds, summer tanagers, brown thrashers, hairy woodpeckers. Fruit of other species appeals to towhees. Mockingbirds, thrashers, towhees scout for good nesting sites.

Deciduous and evergreen large shrubs or small trees. Grow rapidly into dense, tough plants needing little upkeep; even tolerate heat and wind. Flowers are small and inconspicuous, but usually are fragrant, followed by decorative fruits.

E. angustifolia. Russian olive. Small deciduous tree. Zones 3-9. Not only abuse resistant, it is also good looking. Narrow, willowlike silvery gray leaves are in pleasing contrast to dark brown, shredding bark. In winter angular trunk and branches present an attractive pattern. Fruits are yellowish and resemble olives. Wide spreading and rather open, can be trained into 20-foot tree, left to grow as large shrub, or planted in groups as windbreak hedge or screen. Fast growing and vigorous in poorest, dryest soils and in hot, dry regions. Seems out of place in mild-winter, cool-summer climates when compared to lush, broad-leafed evergreens that reach their best development there.

E. commutata. Silverberry or Wolfberry. Deciduous shrub. Zones 3-8. Everything about this plant is silvery: leaves, stems, flowers, and fruits. Leaves are oval, to 4 inches long, on an 8 to 12-foot, fairly upright shrub.

E. multiflora. Cherry elaeagnus. Deciduous. Zones 5-9. Vigorous, spreading shrub to 9 feet high. Noticeably two-tone foliage is dark green above, silver beneath. Leaves are narrowly oval to 3 inches long. Elongated, cherrylike fruits ripen early in summer, before most other fruits.

E. pungens. Thorny elaeagnus. Evergreen. Zones 7-10. Left alone, a rather rigid, sprawling, angular shrub to 6 to 15 feet tall, but pruning will keep it lower and more dense. Silvery gray-green leaves (3 inches long) have wavy edges and many small rusty dots on the surface; spiny branches also have these dots. Overall color effect is olive drab. Spring fruits are brown but later turn red. Several variegated forms are sold, their leaves marked with yellow or white. A similar, but more silvery than gray species is *E. fruitlandii.*

E. umbellata. Autumn elaeagnus. Deciduous. Zones 4-9. Twelve-foot, spreading shrub similar (except for size) to *E. angustifolia.* Oblong, 3-inch leaves are green above, silver beneath. Brown to red berries in fall.

ERIOBOTRYA japonica. LOQUAT

Fall blossoms attract hummingbirds. Mockingbirds, house finches, northern orioles attracted to large-seeded yellow fruits. March to April ripening fruits in desert regions are food for cardinals, curve-billed thrashers, gilded flickers.

Evergreen tree. Zones 8-10. Big, leathery leaves (6 to 12 inches long and up to 4 inches wide) are stoutly veined and netted; glossy and deep green on top, they show rust-colored wool underneath. New branches and flower stalks also are woolly. Tree is quite dense, reaching 15 to 30 feet tall and as wide in sun; more slender in shade. Requires well-drained soil and abundant moisture until it becomes established; later will take some drought but always performs better with moisture. Small white flowers in fall develop into 1 to 2-inch yellow to orange fruits in spring.

EUCALYPTUS

A number of different birds visit eucalyptus trees. To the flowers come hummingbirds, black-headed grosbeaks, orioles, and warblers. Orioles and flickers find some insects. Tanagers, orioles, and juncos may select plant for nesting. Sapsuckers and woodpeckers may be found probing trunks and limbs.

Evergreen trees and shrubs. Native Australian plants perfectly adapted to many parts of California and Arizona. The many species encompass a great variety of sizes and growth habits: from giant windbreak types (*E. globulus, E. viminalis*) to tall and wispy sorts (*E. citriodora*), round-headed flowering trees (*E. ficifolia*), and sprawling shrubs (*E. macrocarpa*). Some species are noted for their attractive plant structure, colorful flowers, unusual or striking foliage, or combinations of these attributes. Nearly all eucalyptus are fast growing and drought tolerant. The following list includes a few of the smaller species that could be used in the average small to moderate-sized garden.

E. calophylla. Zones 9-10. Tree to 50 feet, round headed. Broad, oval leaves (4 to 7 inches long) and rough, fissured bark. Foot-long clusters of white, rose, or red flowers on and off throughout year.

E. citriodora. Lemon-scented gum. Zones 9-10. Tree, 50 to 75 feet; slender, very open and graceful. Chalk white trunk and branches; long (to 7 inches), narrow, yellow-green leaves. Branching begins halfway up the trunk or higher. Whitish, inconspicuous flowers in winter.

E. cornuta. Yate. Zones 9-10. Tree, 35 to 60 feet; spreading, dense crown casts good shade. Leaves (3 to 6 inches long) are shiny green, lance shaped. Summer flowers are greenish yellow in small clusters.

E. ficifolia. Red-flowering gum. Zones 9-10. Tree, to 40 feet, round headed and compact (but also can be large, multi-stemmed shrub). Broadly oval leaves (3 to 7 inches long) thick and shiny deep green. Showy, foot-long flower clusters; blooms usually red but can be orange, salmon, light pink, or cream.

E. grossa. Coarse-flowered mallee. Zones 9-10. Shrub, 9 to 15 feet, usually multi-trunked and spreading. Broadly oval leaves (to 3 inches long) are thick and shining deep green. Spring and summer clusters of yellow flowers are showy against clean green foliage.

E. gunnii. Cider gum. Zones 7 or 8-10. Tree, 40 to 75 feet, vertical and dense. Lance-shaped, 3 to 5-inch leaves. Green and tan bark is smooth. Small creamy white flowers in spring.

E. lehmannii. Bushy yate. Zones 9-10. Tree, 20 to 30 feet; dense, flat topped, and wide spreading. Oval leaves (to 2 inches) are light green; some turn red in fall. Bark is brown. Large clusters of apple green flowers.

E. leucoxylon. White ironbark. Zones 8 or 9-10. Tree, 20 to 80 feet; usually slender, upright and open with drooping branches. Sickle-shaped leaves (3 to 6 inches long) are gray-green. Old bark sheds to reveal white or mottled white trunk. White flowers in winter and spring (variety 'Rosea' has pink blossoms).

E. l. macrocarpa 'Rosea'. Shrub-tree, 15 to 25 feet. Leaves are gray-green, trunk gray to pinkish. Heavy crop of bright red flowers.

E. linearis. White peppermint. Zones 9-10. Tree, 20 to 50 feet; irregular to round-headed, weeping branches. Very narrow, long, dark green leaves; bark is white to light tan, peels off in thin strips. Clusters of creamy white flowers from late spring to fall. Sometimes sold as *E. pulchella, E. amygdalina angustifolia.*

E. macrocarpa. Zones 8-10. Shrub, 4 to 15 feet, sprawling and almost vinelike. Leaves light gray-blue, round but with distinct point, set close to stem; bark is greenish white. Very showy flowers (each 4 to 7 inches across) grow directly on branches; color usually pink but may be red, cream, or white. Doesn't require regular watering.

E. maculosa. Red-spotted gum. Zones 9-10. Tree, 20 to 50 feet; tall, slender, with gracefully drooping branches. Narrow, light grayish green leaves (4 to 6 inches long); bark is brown or gray, flaking off to show powdery white undersurface. Inconspicuous pale flowers.

E. melliodora. Zones 9-10. Tree, 30 to 100 feet, upright with slightly weeping branches. Leaves curving, grayish green (2 to 6 inches long); bark is tan, flaky. Fragrant, inconspicuous flowers in late winter, spring; variety 'Rosea' is pink flowered.

E. microtheca. Zones 7 or 8-10. Tree, 35 to 40 feet, bushy and round headed, single or multi-trunked. Leaves blue-green, ribbonlike (to 8 inches long). Insignificant creamy white flowers.

(Continued on next page)

Eucalyptus rhodantha *is one of the shrubby eucalypts noted for its large and bright red blossoms.*

E. polyanthemos. Silver dollar gum. Zones 8 or 9-10. Tree, 20 to 60 feet, single or multi-trunked. Juvenile leaves round or oval (2 to 3 inches long), mature leaves lance shaped; both are silvery gray. Creamy white flowers in spring and summer.

E. rhodantha. Zones 8-10. Sprawling shrub 4 to 8 feet across. Generally similar to *E. macrocarpa* but growth is less stiff; flowers are slightly smaller and nearly always red. Requires sunny location and little water.

E. sideroxylon. Red or Pink ironbark. Zones 9-10. Tree, 20 to 80 feet; variable habit — open or dense, slender or squatty, weeping or upright. Slender blue-green leaves (turn bronze in winter); rough, nearly black trunk. Flowers light pink to pink-red (usually darker-foliaged plants have darker flowers); bloom is fall through spring. Often sold as *E. s.* 'Rosea'.

EUONYMUS

Ripening fruits draw eastern bluebirds, hermit thrushes, mockingbirds, common flickers, fox sparrows, yellow-rumped warblers, scarlet tanagers, yellow-bellied sapsuckers.

Deciduous or evergreen shrubs. Deciduous species offer spectacular displays of autumn foliage color and bright ripening fruits. Evergreen species listed here have decorative fruit in fall. Growth is vigorous in nearly all garden soils. In some parts of the country, euonymus scale is a serious pest, particularly on evergreen varieties. Check with your local nurseryman or county agricultural agent about its likelihood in your area.

E. alata. Winged euonymus, Spindle tree. Deciduous. Zones 4-9. Horizontal branches build up to dense, twiggy shrub 10 to 12 feet high and to about 15 feet wide. Distinctive feature is flat, corky ridges on younger growth (it disappears on older stems). Dark green, oval leaves turn bright rose-red to scarlet in autumn. Bright orange-red fruits ripen at the same time, but they're not especially conspicuous because of brilliant foliage. The variety 'Compacta' grows only 4 to 6 feet tall and as wide.

E. americana. Strawberry bush. Deciduous. Zones 4-9. Pinkish red, pebbly fruits (somewhat resembling strawberries) open in fall to display orange seeds. Upright growth reaches about 7 feet. Oval leaves (to 4 inches) turn brilliant red in fall.

E. bungeana semipersistens. Winterberry euonymus. Semi-deciduous. Zones 5-9. Fast grower to 18 feet; rather open with light green leaves but no distinctive autumn color. Yellowish fruits hang on for some time after leaves fall.

E. europaea. European spindle tree. Deciduous. Zones 4-9. Growth is to about 20 feet, sometimes treelike. Oblong, 4-inch leaves turn purplish red in fall and hang on for some time before dropping. Fruit is pink, on hanging stems, opening to display orange seeds. Variety 'Aldenhamensis' is somewhat smaller, with more brilliant autumn foliage and fruit.

E. fortunei 'Vegeta'. Big-leaf winter creeper. Evergreen. Zones 6-9. Although it will grow vinelike if planted against a support, when planted in the open it grows into an irregular, mounding shrub. Rich green, 2-inch, oval leaves. Autumn fruits are orange seeds; are revealed when pinkish capsules ripen and open.

E. kiautschovica. Spreading euonymus. Semi-evergreen. Zones 7-9. May be sold under the name *E. patens*. A 9-foot, spreading shrub with light green, 2 to 3-inch leaves. Autumn fruits are showy, pinkish capsules opening to show red seeds.

FAGUS grandifolia. AMERICAN BEECH

Good tree for nesting sites. Attracts robins, vireos, northern orioles, rose-breasted grosbeaks, yellow warblers. Beech nuts liked by several species of grosbeaks, northern flickers, titmice, nuthatches, blue jays, variety of woodpeckers (including red-breasted, downy, and hairy).

Deciduous tree. Zones 4-10. Strikingly beautiful tree for larger properties. Shallow, fibrous root system makes it difficult to grow other plants, lawns underneath. Because lower branches sweep the ground it can be maintained as gigantic pyramidal shrub to about 90 feet. Dense foliage turns golden bronze in autumn; bark is gray.

FICUS. EDIBLE FIG

In some species fruit attracts variety of birds: western bluebirds, house finches, black-headed grosbeaks, mockingbirds, gray catbirds, orioles, yellow-rumped warblers, Swainson's thrushes, towhees, jays, ruby-throated hummingbirds, brown thrashers, robins, starlings, tanagers, waxwings, some woodpeckers. Desert species favored by gilded flickers, cactus wrens, cardinals, curve-billed thrashers. Often used as a roosting site by winter-visiting birds.

Deciduous tree. Zones 5-10. Low-branched, spreading tree with smooth, gray, and gnarled limbs. Rough, lobed, bright green leaves (4 to 9 inches long and nearly as wide) have tropical appearance. Shade is dense. Avoid deep cultivation (may damage surface roots) and high nitrogen fertilizers (stimulate growth at expense of fruit). Plants are self-fertile; most varieties produce two crops a year. Varieties differ in climate adaptability; check with local nurseryman for kinds best suited to your area.

FRAXINUS. Ash

Provides flat-winged seeds. Attracts purple finches, evening and pine grosbeaks, cedar waxwings, bobwhites. Yellow-bellied sapsuckers often drill for sap.

Deciduous trees. Most are too large for average suburban gardens. As street trees or in highly manicured gardens, they have reputation of being messy. Where male and female trees are planted together, large quantities of easily germinating seeds are produced; can be a litter problem.

F. americana. White ash. Zones 4-9. Rapid growth to 80 feet or more, with straight trunk and oval-shaped crown. Dark green leaves are 8 to 15 inches long, each consisting of 5 to 9 leaflets. Autumn color may be purple or yellow.

F. holotricha. Zones 6-10. Smaller in all respects than *F. americana.* Slender, upright tree to 40 feet; casts light shade. Yellow fall color.

F. latifolia. Oregon ash. Zones 7-10. Upright growth to 40 to 80 feet; leaves are light green. Tolerates standing in water during winter.

F. pensylvanica. Green ash. Zones 3-8. Moderate growth reaches 30 to 60 feet; forms compact, oval crown. Light green foliage burns in hot, dry winds. Autumn color is yellow.

FUCHSIA

Hummingbirds like simple, single-flowered kinds (they have a hard time getting beaks into big, complex, double flowers). Large, bushy plants give good shelter for bushtits.

Evergreen to deciduous shrubs (nearly evergreen in mildest climates). Flowers are bright and showy, whether inch-long or nearly fist size. All fuchsias are easy to grow if provided with regular water; the leaves wilt quickly if soil becomes too dry. Plants grow exuberantly if fertilized often. Best growth is where summers are cool and atmosphere moist. Where summers are warm, windy, dry, or sunny, protect plants from wind and give them all-day filtered sunlight, frequent overhead sprinkling.

F. arborescens. Zones 9-10. Shrub to 18 feet tall with 8-inch leaves. Small, pinkish to purplish flowers come in erect clusters (unlike most other fuchsias which have drooping flowers).

F. fulgens. Zones 9-10. A 4-foot (or sometimes more) shrub with oval leaves to 7 inches long. Firecracker-like, 3-inch-long flowers come in drooping clusters.

F. hybrida. Zones 9-10. Can be grown as container plants in colder zones if placed in cool porch or greenhouse. These are the common, flamboyant fuchsias with the largest flowers. Countless named hybrids are sold, and they vary greatly in color combinations, flower form, and growth habit. Many plants are shrubby, others are trailing and look best in hanging containers. Plants will continue to flower from spring well into fall if you water and fertilize regularly and remove the berries that form after flowers fall.

F. magellanica. Zones 6-10. Vigorous, arching shrub averaging 4 to 6 feet tall, although can get much higher in favorable mild regions especially when trained against a wall. Flowers (1½ inches long) are red and purple. In coldest regions of its adaptability, mound up base of plant with soil or sawdust to insure survival of roots over winter.

GARRYA. Silktassel

Birds supplementing their diets with purplish berries are bushtits, chestnut-backed chickadees, wrentits, California thrashers, California quail, mockingbirds, brown towhees.

Evergreen shrubs. Most distinctive feature is long, decorative catkins appearing on male plants in winter; female plants have much shorter, far less showy catkins. Female plants produce purplish berries, but both male and female plants are needed to get fruit.

G. elliptica. Coast silktassel. Zones 8-9. Large shrub or small tree. Densely foliaged; will grow in sun or part shade. Withstands summer heat and tolerates summer watering. Elliptical leaves are 2½ inches long, wavy edged, dark green above, gray-woolly beneath.

G. fremontii. Fremont silktassel. Zones 7-9. Similar in appearance to *G. elliptica*, but has glossy, yellow-green leaves that have smooth edges and are not woolly underneath. More tolerant of drought, heat, and cold; grows best in full sun.

HETEROMELES arbutifolia. Toyon

Clusters of red berries ripen in late fall, attracting common flickers, wrentits, robins, house and purple finches, cedar waxwings, mockingbirds, California quail, bluebirds, grosbeaks, tanagers, thrashers, thrushes, titmice, brown towhees.

Evergreen. Zones 8-10. Large, dense shrub around 10 feet tall, or small tree to 25 feet if given plenty of water. Leaves are thick, glossy dark green with toothed edges — to 4 inches long and up to an inch wide. In late spring produces small white flowers in flattish clusters 4 to 6 inches across; flowers set small berries that ripen bright red in late autumn. Drought tolerant, but thrives with summer water in well-drained soil; needs summer water in desert regions.

HOLODISCUS discolor. CREAM BUSH

When in bloom, mass of flowers attract insects; insects eaten by bushtits, chickadees, warblers, fox sparrows, towhees. Hummingbirds favor blossom nectar. Favored by wrens in northwestern regions.

Deciduous shrub. Zones 4-8. Native to western states as far east as Rocky Mountains. May grow to 20 feet in moist soil and part shade but will reach only 3 to 4 feet in dry, sunny situations. Triangular leaves (to 3 inches long) are deep green above, white and hairy below, with coarsely toothed edges. Has showy, nodding clusters (up to 12 inches long) of creamy white flowers in spring to early summer; fade to tannish gold and brown.

ILEX. HOLLY

Fruit eaters flock to berries. Birds most often seen are red-headed woodpeckers, bobwhites, mockingbirds, northern flickers, gray catbirds, brown thrashers, cedar waxwings, yellow-bellied sapsuckers, sparrows, starlings. Returning each year to fill up on berries of I. decidua are bobwhites, mockingbirds, robins, hermit thrushes, brown thrashers, gray catbirds, northern flickers, eastern bluebirds, cedar waxwings. Dense, prickly foliage provides good nesting sites for mockingbirds, thrashers, towhees.

Evergreen or deciduous shrubs or trees. Most are slow to moderate growers that function as shrubs for years.

Ilex aquifolium *(English holly) doesn't always have spiny green leaves with red berries.* **Above:** *a variety with spines only at leaf tips.* **Right:** *variety 'Fructo-luteo' has yellow berries.*

Some grow to tree height and bulk. Unless otherwise noted, hollies bear male and female flowers on separate plants; to get berries on female plant you must have male plant nearby (not necessarily of same species, but must bloom at same time as female plant). Hollies prefer good garden soil (slightly acid) kept moist but with good drainage.

I. aquifolium. English holly. Evergreen shrub or tree. Zones 7-9. Typical holly leaf with spiny-edged, dark green leaves. Highly variable in leaf shape, color, and degree of spininess, resulting in hundreds of named varieties sold (including those with variegated leaves). Some of selected foliage forms are strictly male plants; are useless as source of food for birds. Slow growth eventually produces pyramidal tree (or huge shrub) of 40 feet or more. Needs protection from sun in hot, dry areas.

I. aquipernyi 'Brilliant'. Evergreen shrub. Zones 7-10. Dense, conical shrub to 10 feet or more; will produce heavy berry crop without pollination. Leaves grow to 4 inches long with few but very pronounced teeth.

I. cassine. Dahoon. Evergreen. Zones 8-9. May become small tree over 20 feet tall, but is easily kept lower. Leaves are oblong, 2 to 5 inches in length, with or without toothed margins; winter color is purplish green. Red berries in winter are profuse on growth of the current year. In native region it grows in wet soils.

I. cornuta. Chinese holly. Evergreen shrub or small tree. Zones 7-10. Dense to open growth will reach about 10 feet high and wide. Typical leaves are glossy, leathery, and nearly rectangular with spines at four corners and tip. Berries are nearly ½ inch in diameter but plant needs a long warm season to set fruit. Many named varieties of this species are sold; the following will produce berries without a nearby male plant for pollination: 'Burfordii', the Burford holly; 'Burfordii Nana', smaller, more compact, and slower growing; 'Dazzler'; 'Femina'; 'Giant Beauty'; 'Newport'; and 'Tustin'.

I. crenata. Japanese holly. Evergreen shrub. Zones 6-10. Looks less like a holly than do most species. Narrow, finely toothed leaves are less than an inch long; berries are black. Usually dense, erect plant under 10 feet tall; good substitute for boxwood in regions too cold for the latter. Variety 'Convexa' is excellent for

hedges, growing only 4 to 6 feet tall but spreading wider.

I. decidua. Possum-haw. Deciduous. Zones 6-10. Large shrub with oval, toothed leaves to about 4 inches long. Large berries (to ½ inch in diameter) are red or orange-red.

I. glabra. Inkberry. Evergreen shrub, but only semi-evergreen in colder zones of its adaptability. Zones 4-9. Black-berried holly but not as dense or polished as *I. crenata.* Leaves are about 2 inches long, glossy and dark green, oval but broader toward the tip. Grows to about 6 feet tall. Native to swampy areas but also will succeed in fairly dry soils.

I. latifolia. Lusterleaf holly. Evergreen tree. Zones 7-10. Slow growing with stout branches; may reach 50 to 60 feet tall. Leaves are largest among hollies (6 to 8 inches long); are dark green, thick and leathery, with finely toothed edges. Large, dull red berries are borne in large clusters. Prefers some shade.

I. opaca. American holly. Evergreen tree. Zones 6-9. Slow growing, eventually pyramidal form to 50 feet. Leaves (2 to 4 inches long) have spiny margins, are dull or glossy green. Like *I. aquifolium,* is highly variable, and numerous varieties have been named.

I. verticillata. Black alder, Winterberry. Deciduous shrub. Zones 4-9. In native swamps may reach 15 feet or more, but in ordinary garden soils seldom exceeds 10 feet. Oval, dark green leaves (to 3 inches long) turn yellow in autumn at same time small berries become red; leaves then fall but berries remain on bare, gray-twigged plant.

I. vomitoria. Yaupon. Evergreen. Zones 7-10. Large shrub or small tree in the 15 to 20-foot range. Narrow, inch-long leaves are dark green with wavy toothed edges. Tiny scarlet berries are produced without a pollinator. Tolerates extreme alkaline soils better than other hollies.

JUNIPERUS. Juniper

Good nesting and shelter sites. Variety of birds gather the seeds or fruits. Favoring the J. occidentalis are solitaires, evening grosbeaks, mockingbirds. Evening and pine grosbeaks, purple finches, robins, Swainson's thrushes, bobwhites like the J. scopulorum. Partial to the J. virginiana are more than 54 species, including common flickers, mockingbirds, robins, evening and pine grosbeaks, purple finches, eastern bluebirds, yellow-rumped warblers, cedar waxwings, tree swallows, phoebes, cardinals, eastern kingbirds. Northwestern junipers attract jays.

Evergreen shrubs and trees. In most cases, berry-bearing female plants are separate from male plants. If you want to plant for fruit, plants of both sexes are needed. Simplest way of making sure you get female plant is to buy one that already has fruit. All tree forms are strongly upright, generally pyramidal, and fairly slow growing. Drought resistant. Soil tolerance is quite wide (except water-logged soil).

(Continued on next page)

Juniperus scopulorum (Rocky mountain juniper) left, forms dense pyramid in youth. **Above:** *typical juniper berries feed many different bird species.*

J. chinensis. Chinese juniper. Tree. Zones 5-10. Wild species seldom is sold; nurseries offer vast number of selected forms under various names. Growth habits differ (columnar, shorter and broader, for example) and colors range from silvery and bluish types through shades of green.

J. deppeana pachyphlaea. Alligator juniper. Zones 7-10. Native to Southwest. May ultimately reach 60 feet; otherwise is shrubby, somewhat spreading. Foliage is blue-gray; bark is strikingly checked like alligator hide.

J. occidentalis. Western juniper, Yellow cedar. Zones 5-10. Native to west coast where it develops into round-headed tree of 40 feet.

J. scopulorum. Rocky Mountain juniper. Zones 6-10. In dry climates it is better choice than *J. virginiana.* Narrow to eventually round-topped tree of about 35 feet. Many named growth and color forms are sold.

J. virginiana. Eastern red cedar. Zones 3-10. Dense pyramid or column, broadening somewhat as it matures to 50 feet or more. Native east of Rocky Mountains and better there than two preceding species.

LANTANA camara

Long flowering and fruiting season produces clusters of blackish berries for these fruit eaters: house finches, robins, mockingbirds, California quail, thrashers, jays. Winter flowers attract hummingbirds, yellow-rumped warblers.

Evergreen shrub. Zones 9-10. Six-foot, irregular to rounded shrub with rough, dark green leaves and prickly, hairy stems. Individual flowers are tiny, but come in closely packed clusters 1 to 1½ inches across — a mixture of yellow, orange, and red. In nurseries you're more likely to find named hybrids of this species that are smaller (2 to 4 feet, usually), more compact shrubs. Their colors may be white, cream, yellow, orange, red, pink, or combinations of two or more of these shades — depending on the variety. Each tiny flower produces a small, purplish black berry combining to form a blackberrylike fruit cluster.

LARIX. Larch

Seeds from small cones eaten by American goldfinches, purple finches, pine siskins, red-breasted nuthatches.

Deciduous conifers. Among cone-bearing trees, larches are nearly unique in deciduous habit. Autumn color is bright yellow; new spring needles (½ to 1½ inches long) are soft light green. Slender pyramidal shape with horizontal branches and drooping branchlets; winter interest is enhanced by many small cones, creating polka dot pattern against the sky. Not particular as to soil; will accept lawn watering. In some regions require protection from worm that eats needles before they emerge from their cases in spring.

L. decidua. European larch. Zones 3-9. Moderate to fast growth to 30 to 60 feet. Summer color is grass green, lighter than other species.

L. laricina. American larch, Tamarack. Zones 3-8. Sixty-foot tree not suitable for low altitudes in the West. In the East grows well only as far south as West Virginia.

L. leptolepis. Japanese larch. Zones 5-9. Rapid growth to 60 feet or more. Summer color is soft bluish green.

LIGUSTRUM. Privet

Berries occasionally eaten by bobwhites, quail, bluebirds, purple finches, cedar waxwings, towhees, goldfinches, house finches, mockingbirds.

Deciduous and evergreen shrubs. Most people think of privets as hedges — and they do lend themselves very well to that function. But usually a closely clipped privet hedge is too dense for most birds to enter, and because it loses most of its flowering wood, it cannot produce fruits. If you want to use privets for hedging, keep as an informal, unclipped green wall by only cutting back branches that stray markedly from overall pattern. Any of the species listed here make good looking single shrubs. All have abundant, showy clusters of white to creamy white flowers in late spring or early summer; small blue-black, berrylike fruits follow them. Most privets grow easily in sun or in some shade, and in any soil. For best growth and appearance, water them regularly.

L. amurense. Amur privet. Semi-evergreen. Zones 4-9. Upright and rather pyramidal shrub (10 to 15 feet) similar to *L. ovalifolium,* but definitely hardier. Oval leaves are 1½ to 2½ inches long.

L. ibolium. Ibolium privet. Deciduous. Zones 5-9. Also similar to *L. ovalifolium* and is considered to be more attractive than *L. amurense* but is less cold tolerant. Dark green, glossy leaves.

L. japonicum. Japanese or Waxleaf privet. Evergreen. Zones 7-10. In nursery trade often mixed with *L. lucidum.* Ten to 12-foot dense shrub with 2 to 4-inch leaves, glossy on their upper sides but much paler to nearly white beneath. Slightly spongy to the touch. It makes neat, untrimmed hedge. *L. lucidum* (Glossy privet) can grow into a 35-foot tree; its leaves are 4 to 6 inches long, glossy on both sides, and leathery feeling but not spongy. Plants sold as *L. texanum* are variety 'Texanum' of *L. japonicum* — lower growing (6 to 9 feet) and more dense.

L. lucidum. Glossy privet. Evergreen. See *L. japonicum.*

L. obtusifolium. Border privet. Evergreen. Zones 4-10. Arching growth reaches 6 to 10 feet. Leaves are oblong, to 2½ inches, turning purplish or brown-tinted purple in autumn. Variety 'Regelianum' (Regel's privet) grows only 4 to 5 feet high; has distinctive horizontal branching pattern.

L. ovalifolium. California privet. Semi-deciduous; evergreen only in mildest areas. Zones 7-10. Rapid, compact growth to 15 feet with glossy dark green, oval leaves to 2½ inches long. Commonly used as hedge plant. Root system is shallow and greedy.

L. vulgare. Common privet. Deciduous. Zones 5-10. Broad plant to 15 feet tall; often used as hedge plant. Root system is less greedy than *L. ovalifolium.* Subject to blight in some parts of the country; check with your county agricultural agent or local nurseryman before planting.

LINDERA benzoin. SPICE BUSH

Fruits attract thrushes, vireos. Other birds also enjoying fruits are eastern kingbirds, robins, mockingbirds, cardinals, eastern bluebirds, gray catbirds, common flickers.

Deciduous shrub. Zones 5-8. Dense, twiggy plant 6 to 15 feet tall and just as wide. Before leaves appear in spring, tiny greenish yellow flowers appear along the branches. Like hollies, some plants have only male flowers, others only female; where the two grow together, the female plant will have bright red, ½-inch berries in fall. Bright green leaves are 3 to 5 inches long, turn brilliant yellow in autumn. Best in moist soils; neutral to acid soil preferred.

LIQUIDAMBAR styraciflua. AMERICAN SWEET GUM

Seeds inside ball-shaped fruits supplement diet of cardinals, bobwhites, mourning doves, dark-eyed juncos, bushtits, white-throated sparrows, American goldfinches, black-capped chickadees, purple finches. Tree is often engraved by yellow-bellied sapsuckers.

Deciduous tree. Zones 6-10. Slender and cone shaped in youth, always much taller than wide in maturity (may be up to 125 feet in native eastern states, around 60 feet in cultivation). Growth rate is moderate. Leaves are lobed and very maplelike, color beautifully in autumn — yellow, orange, all shades of red, depending on the individual tree. Several named selections are sold, singled out chiefly for dependable fall color. Requires good garden soil that is neutral to slightly acid. Very effective when planted in groves. Fruit is ball shaped, containing many seeds; remains on tree after leaves fall.

LIRIODENDRON tulipifera. TULIP TREE

Flowers attract hummingbirds. Seeds eaten by cardinals, purple finches, evening grosbeaks. Yellow-bellied sapsuckers frequently puncture upper branches to get sap.

Deciduous tree. Zones 5-9. Fast growth to 60 to 80 feet (well over 100 feet in native eastern states). Spreads eventually to about half its height. Trunk is rigidly straight with pyramidal crown of foliage. Not suited to small gardens because of size and spreading root system. Tulip-shaped, 2-inch-wide blooms are greenish yellow with orange bases, appearing in late spring after tree has leafed out. Prefers neutral to slightly acid soil and plenty of summer water. Good yellow fall color, even in mild climates.

LONICERA. HONEYSUCKLE

Great favorite of most birds. Insect eaters like blossoms. Hummingbirds like flower nectar. Berrylike fruits eaten by variety of birds: gray catbirds, robins, brown thrashers, cedar waxwings, hermit thrushes, pine grosbeaks, solitaires, towhees, wrentits, bluebirds, chickadees, finches. L. fragrantissima is favorite nesting place for gray catbirds, mockingbirds, song sparrows, cardinals.

Deciduous and evergreen shrubs. In addition to their bird-attracting fruits, shrubby honeysuckles have numerous other features: they are vigorous and easy to grow, tolerate many different soils (except wet ones), have showy flowers and fruits, and generally are good looking landscape subjects.

L. bella. Belle honeysuckle. Deciduous. Zones 5-10. A hybrid group, derived from crossing *L. morrowi* and *L. tatarica.* Both pink and white flowered forms are available. Fairly upright growth to 6 feet with 2-inch, oval leaves. Small red berries in early summer.

L. fragrantissima. Winter honeysuckle. Deciduous, partly evergreen in mild-winter areas. Zones 6-10. Fragrant, white blossoms appear very early in spring; red berries also ripen early, usually before summer. Flowers are not showy, and the berries often are somewhat concealed by new growth. Arching, rather stiff stems may reach 8 feet; oval, 1 to 3-inch leaves are dull dark green above, blue-green beneath.

L. involucrata. Twinberry. Deciduous. Zones 4-10. Densely foliaged. Grows 5 to 10 feet tall with 2 to 5-inch, oval, dark green leaves. Yellowish flowers appear in pairs, followed by two berries side-by-side that appear red but ripen black. Flowering is from early spring to early summer.

(Continued on next page)

KEEPING PART OF YOUR FRUIT CROP

No matter how alluring you make your garden with plants that specifically attract birds, some birds are certain to zero in on some of the fruits that you may have planted just for your consumption. Particular favorites are the cane berries (blackberries, raspberries, and their relatives), blueberries, cherries, and grapes. Even larger fruits, such as apples, figs, and plums or prunes, may be partially eaten by some birds.

In order to keep your share of those food crops, you can choose from these three general courses of action: grow decoy food plants, net or cage the fruits you want to save, or put out some sort of device to scare off the birds.

Decoy fruits. Because cultivated fruits ripen at different times (there are, for example, early, midseason, and late ripening blueberries), what you plant as a decoy fruit depends upon what fruit — and what variety of it — you are growing for your use. For the best advice in your locality, check with the nearest county agricultural agent or University Agricultural Extension Service.

Covering the fruits. You have several choices of protective covering for fruiting plants. Cheesecloth and black (or green) nylon netting is often sold by agricultural supply stores (feed and grain shops, in rural areas), or your nurseryman may be able to order them for you. A more recent material is a vinyl-coated and mildew-proof paper fabric that has ½-inch-square mesh, lasting for two to three years. For the gardener who is handy with a hammer and nails, there is the option of a wooden-framed "cage" covered with netting, screening, or ½-inch poultry netting.

Scaring devices. A stuffed hawk scarecrow placed in the branches of a tree will provide some degree of protection for your crop. Other devices you can hang in trees are fluttering pieces of glass, colored feathers, shiny tops from tin cans, or jar lids — dangled from string stretched around the perimeter of trees or shrubs. Because birds quickly become accustomed to any one device, keep a varying arsenal of scare devices on hand that can be changed every few days.

. . . Lonicera (cont'd.)

L. korolkowii. Blue-leaf honeysuckle. Deciduous. Zones 6-10. Large, arching plant to 12 feet tall and as wide or wider. Oval, 2-inch leaves are distinctively blue-green. Profusion of small, rose-colored flowers in mid-spring is followed by many bright red fruits in summer or early fall. Will perform well in desert heat. Plants sometimes are hard to establish. Variety 'Zabelii' is smaller, has broader leaves, deeper rose flowers.

L. maackii. Amur honeysuckle. Deciduous, but leaves hang on until late fall or early winter. Zones 3-9. In late spring, after most honeysuckles have bloomed, this species opens its fragrant white flowers, which turn yellow as they age. Dark red berries ripen in fall while leaves are still green. Grows 12 to 15 feet high and about as wide.

L. morrowii. Morrow honeysuckle. Deciduous. Zones 4-9. Dense, rounded, and spreading growth produces plant to 6 feet tall and up to twice as wide. White flowers yellow with age, are followed by dark red berries in summer. Leaves are gray-green, oblong to about 3 inches.

L. nitida. Box honeysuckle. Evergreen. Zones 7-10. Dense, leafy branches form an erect, 6-foot-high plant; individual leaves are shiny and dark green but only ½-inch long. Fragrant, creamy white flowers in late spring produce blue-purple berries in fall. Easily trained as hedge. A good seashore plant, as it withstands salt spray.

L. pileata. Privet honeysuckle. Semi-evergreen. Zones 6-10. Leaves are small, oval, dark green, and glossy. Purple berries in autumn come from small, fragrant, white spring flowers. Grows to about 4 feet with horizontal branching pattern.

L. tatarica. Tatarian honeysuckle. Deciduous. Zones 3-9. Big, upright, dense mass of twiggy branches to 9 feet tall covered with oval, 2-inch-long, dark green or bluish green leaves. Summer-ripening fruits are bright red. Several varieties are sold, with white or pink flowers. White-flowered forms do not yellow with age. All are neat plants for background or screen plantings.

MAGNOLIA

Variety of birds eat flowers and fruits. Often visiting M. grandiflora are gray catbirds, common flickers, mockingbirds, robins, brown thrashers, red-eyed vireos, red-bellied woodpeckers. M. virginiana attracts eastern kingbirds, mockingbirds, robins, wood thrushes, red-eyed vireos.

Evergreen or deciduous trees. Of the many magnolia species and hybrids available, the two species listed in the next column are chosen for their density.

M. grandiflora. Southern magnolia. Evergreen. Zones 7-10. Dense, pyramidal to round-headed shape; may reach 80 feet with spread half as wide. Big, oval leaves are dark green with lacquerlike finish. Throughout summer it bears famous white blossoms, evoking images of gracious southern plantations. Flowers (8 to 10 inches across) have about six boat-shaped, heavy petals, and powerful fragrance. Requires moist but well-drained, good garden soil (preferably neutral to slightly acid) and plenty of organic matter at planting time. Succeeds in desert regions if protected from wind.

M. virginiana. Sweet bay. Zones 6-10. Evergreen tree to 60 feet tall, growing in wet to almost swampy soils. Native to southeastern states. Grown farther north (within hardiness range) becomes more shrubby and less evergreen. Leaves (2 to 5 inches long) are grayish green on upper surfaces, nearly white underneath. From June to September bears nearly globular blossoms (2 to 3 inches wide) that are creamy white and fragrant.

MAHONIA

Cedar waxwings, robins, mockingbirds, house finches, brown towhees like fruit. Provides all-year shelter; tall, spiny structure favored for nesting.

Evergreen shrubs. Shrub effect produced by these plants comes from numerous stems sent up from roots. Long leaves along stems are divided into leaflets edged with spiny teeth. Yellow flowers in dense, rounded to spikelike clusters are followed by blue-black, berry-like fruits.

M. aquifolium. Oregon grape. Zones 6-9. May reach 6 feet tall; width increases as plant grows older. Leaves, reaching 10 inches long, are composed of five to nine oval-shaped leaflets each up to 2½ inches long and holly-like with spiny edges. Young growth is bronze colored, becoming bright to dark green; in cold winter climates, it turns purplish to red-bronze. Will take nearly any soil and various amounts of water.

M. bealei. Leatherleaf mahonia. Zones 6-10. Same growth and leaf pattern as *M. aquifolium*, but reaches 10 to 12 feet high. Leaves are over a foot long, and leaflets may be as long as 5 inches — yellowish green above and gray-green below with spiny edges. Prefers part shade except in cool-summer regions; best in good soil with ample water.

M. lomariifolia. Zones 8-10. Mature plants will be clumps of erect, little-branched stems 6 to 10 feet tall. Clustered near the ends of stems are horizontally held leaves (to 2 feet long) composed of numerous thick, spiny green leaflets. Yellow flowers in winter and early spring are followed by powdery blue berries. Best with afternoon shade.

M. nevinii. Nevin mahonia. Zones 8-10. Many-branched shrub 3 to 10 feet tall; gray foliage with 1-inch-long, spiny leaflets; red berries. Takes sun or light shade, any soil, and any amount of water.

MALUS. Apple and crabapple

Apple provides good nesting sites for grosbeaks, robins. Fruit eaten by house and purple finches, gray catbirds, evening and pine grosbeaks, waxwings, red-headed woodpeckers, robins, common flickers. Blossoms often eaten by waxwings, grosbeaks; buds may be eaten by pine grosbeaks. Crabapples eaten by mockingbirds; black-headed, evening, and pine grosbeaks; robins; cedar waxwings; starlings.

Deciduous trees and a few shrubs. Noted for profusion of spring flowers, colorful and often edible fruits. The familiar eating apples are mostly derived from one species *(M. pumila)*; crabapples have a more diverse background.

Apple. Zones 4-9. Growth varies according to variety, but generally is round topped and spreading (up to 40 feet high and wide). Attractive blossoms (to 1½ inches across) in spring are followed by oval, 3-inch leaves. Some varieties are self-fruitful, others need another growing nearby for pollination. Varieties differ in climatic preferences for good fruit production; check with your local nurseryman for best varieties for your area.

Crabapple. Mostly Zones 4-9, although a few are hardier. Bewildering number (over 200) of species, selected species forms, and named hybrids are sold; considerable variety in flower color, time of bloom, fruit size, and color. Flowers can be white, any shade of pink, to red and purplish red; single, semi-double, or double. Some kinds have pink or red flower buds that contrast pleasantly with lighter pink or white blossoms. Range of fruit colors is from yellow through orange shades to red. Many species are most easily grown from seed, which means that there will be some variation even within species. For particular color or fruit, it's best to buy one of the named varieties which are propagated by grafting.

Because crabapples are planted not only for their decoration (generally graceful, rounded, small trees with beautiful show of spring flowers) but also to provide food for birds, it is important to select a species that will consistently bear fruit each year or one bearing fruit well into winter. The following crabapples are most likely to be sold as fruit bearers; those followed by (w) also retain fruit late in season: 'Adams', *atrosanguinea* (w), *baccata* (some forms), 'Blanche Adams', 'Dorothea', 'Flame', 'Gorgeous', 'Henry F. DuPont', 'Katherine' (w), 'Marshal Oyama', 'Ormiston Roy' (w), 'Prince Georges', *purpurea* 'Lemoinei', 'Radiant' (w), 'Rosseau', *scheideckeri*, 'Sissipuk' (w), 'Snowbank' and 'Vanguard'.

Malus sargentii (Sargent crabapple) is a deciduous, dense, broader than tall shrub with zig-zag branching pattern. It's slow growing to about 10 feet. Small but profuse white spring flowers produce tiny red crabapples that hang on well into winter.

Crabapples prefer good, well-drained garden soil, tolerate wet, rocky, and mildly acid or alkaline soils. Fireblight is generally handled by removing affected branches below blighted portion, disinfecting shears between each cut. Cedar rust disease appears only where nearby junipers are also diseased. Where it is troublesome, apple scab seems to seriously affect only the Oriental species.

MELALEUCA

Flower nectar draws hummingbirds. Orioles will feed on nectar and on insects that flowers attract. Insects also are favored by tanagers and migrating warblers.

Evergreen shrubs and trees. Zones 8-10. All melaleucas have narrow leaves; clustered flowers with prominent stamens look like bottlebrushes (for other similar bottlebrush plants, see *Callistemon*, page 60). Most are vigorous and fast growing, taking heat, wind, poor soil, drought, and salt air. As plants of larger species age, they often develop picturesque, contorted branches. The following are some of the most widely sold.

M. armillaris. Drooping melaleuca. Shrub to small tree (15 to 30 feet). Drooping branches of light green, needlelike (1 inch long) leaves that are prickly. Furrowed gray bark. Fluffy white flowers come in spring to fall. Tough and adaptable; good for clipped or unclipped barrier hedges, informal shrub, or small tree with training. Easily withstands ocean winds.

M. elliptica. Shrub or small tree (8 to 15 feet high). Rounded, ½-inch leaves mostly at ends of fanlike branches; bark is brown and shreddy. Has showy red bottlebrushes from early spring to fall.

M. ericifolia. Heath melaleuca. Shrub or small tree (10 to 25 feet). Dark green, needlelike leaves (1 inch long); tan or gray bark is soft and fibrous. Creamy flowers in early spring. Fast growing; tolerates alkaline soil, poor drainage, seashore conditions.

M. hypericifolia. Dotted melaleuca. Shrub (6 to 10 feet tall). Drooping branches of copper green to dull green small leaves. Bright orange-red flowers come in late spring through winter. Takes drought and ocean wind (but not direct salt spray).

M. nesophila. Pink melaleuca. Tree or large shrub; fast growth to 20 feet (or sometimes more). Produces gnarled, heavy branches that sprawl or ascend in picturesque patterns; bark is thick and spongy. Gray-green, rounded leaves (1 inch long). Flowers are lavender-pink fading to white, appear during most of the year. Tough plant: takes ocean wind and salt spray, poor and rocky soils, desert heat, little or much water, and can be sheared as a hedge.

M. quinquenervia. Cajeput tree. Tree, usually sold as *M. leucadendra*. Upright and open, 20 to 40 feet. Trunk has thick, spongy, tan to whitish bark that peels off in sheets. Oval leaves (2 to 4 inches long) are pale green, shiny, turning purple after light frost. Appearing in summer and fall, flowers are usually yellowish white. Takes much or little water.

M. styphelioides. Tree, 20 to 40 feet. Lacy, open growth with drooping branches. Pale bark is thick and spongy, peels off in papery layers. Tiny leaves are light green, prickly. Creamy flowers in summer and fall. Any soil.

MELIA azedarach. CHINA BERRY

Blossoms attract ruby-throated hummingbirds. Berries are eaten by gray catbirds, robins, mockingbirds.

Deciduous tree. Zones 7-10. Weed tree in good soil and benign climates, but good plant in hottest, driest climates and poor, alkaline soil. Also withstands all but strongest ocean winds. Spreading tree to 30 to 50 feet high with 1 to 3-foot-long leaves cut into many 1 to 2-inch-long, narrow leaflets. In early summer bears loose clusters of lilac-colored flowers followed by ½-inch, hard yellow fruits that are popular with birds but otherwise poisonous. Variety most frequently seen is 'Umbraculifera', (Texas umbrella tree). It grows quickly into 30-foot tree with dense, spreading, dome-shaped-to-flat crown. Wood is brittle.

MORUS. MULBERRY

Fruits popular with variety of birds. Most consistent visitors are eastern bluebirds, bobwhites, cardinals, robins, gray catbirds, purple finches, American goldfinches, song sparrows, grosbeaks (black-headed and rose-breasted), blue jays, orioles, mockingbirds, tanagers, brown thrashers, vireos, cedar waxwings, woodpeckers (downy, hairy, red-headed, red-breasted), common flickers, titmice. Desert region mulberries, ripening in May and June to a messy purple fruit, attract curve-billed thrashers, house finches, gilded flickers, Gila woodpeckers.

Deciduous trees. Fast growers (to about 50 feet) with dense, round head and spreading shape. Leaves are bright green (to about 6 inches long), usually lobed, but form, size, and shape are variable — often on a single tree. Avoid planting near patios or walkways: juicy, blackberrylike fallen fruit can cause staining problems; can be tracked to other areas. Adapt to hot, dry deserts with alkaline soil, or even seashore conditions. Drought resistant but grow much better and faster if watered regularly when young. Stake new plants carefully because large crowns develop quickly and may snap from slender young trunks in high winds.

M. alba. White mulberry. Zones 5-10. Oriental native on which silkworms feed. Fruit usually is white, or sometimes pale pink.

M. nigra. Black or Persian mulberry. Zones 7-10. Shorter tree (to 30 feet) with short trunk and dense, spreading head; leaves usually are not lobed. Fruit is large, juicy, and dark red to black.

M. rubra. Red or American mulberry. Zones 6-10. Similar tree to *M. alba* but fruit is red or red-purple.

MYRICA. Wax myrtle

Enjoying fruit of M. californica are common flickers, northern orioles, tree swallows, cedar waxwings, chestnut-backed chickadees, towhees, wrentits, yellow-rumped warblers. Fruit of other wax myrtles attracts tree swallows, white-eyed vireos, myrtle warblers, scrub jays, Carolina wrens, towhees, mockingbirds, brown thrashers, bobwhites, downy woodpeckers, common flickers, robins, finches, tufted titmice.

Evergreen or deciduous shrubs. Neat, undramatic plants with inconspicuous flowers but small, waxy fruits in fall on female plants. Both male and female plants are needed for fruit set.

M. californica. Pacific wax myrtle. Evergreen. Zones 7-10. Large shrub that may become treelike to 30 feet with several trunks. Or you can use it as an informal or clipped hedge from 6 to 25 feet tall. Dense, glossy dark green leaves are very narrow but to 4½ inches long. Fall fruit is purplish.

M. cerifera. Wax myrtle. Evergreen. Zones 7-10. Similar to *M. californica*; has gray fruits, shorter leaves.

M. pensylvanica. Bayberry. Deciduous or semi-evergreen. Zones 3-8. Smaller shrub, to about 9 feet tall; compact and dense. Narrow, 4-inch, glossy green

Myrica pensylvanica (Bayberry) bears silver-gray, waxy berries that are popular winter food for birds.

leaves are dotted with resin glands and have a pungent odor. Tiny gray fruits hang on well into winter. Will take poor, sandy soil.

NYSSA sylvatica. Sour gum, tupelo, pepperidge

Seeds eaten by common flickers, robins, woodpeckers, mockingbirds, Swainson's thrushes, brown thrashers.

Deciduous tree. Zones 5-9. Native to eastern states, particularly in swampy regions. Well adapted to most garden soils; tolerates occasional drought. Native trees may reach 90 feet, but in gardens is slow to moderate grower in 30 to 50-foot range; spread is 15 to 25 feet. Shape is pyramidal when young, becomes more irregular, spreading, and rugged with age. Glossy dark green leaves are 2 to 5 inches long, turning hot, coppery red in autumn; color is dependable even in mild-winter areas. Spring leaf-out is rather late. Only female trees bear small blue berries.

OSTRYA virginiana. Hop-hornbeam

Inflated, small, bladderlike fruits favored by purple finches, downy woodpeckers, rose-breasted grosbeaks.

Deciduous tree. Zones 5-9. Small to medium sized (30 to 40 feet) with pyramidal shape. Leaves are 3 to 5 inches long, oval, and toothed, turning yellow in fall. Fruits are nutlets enclosed in conspicuous bladderlike pods that hang in short clusters.

PHELLODENDRON amurense. Amur cork tree

Mockingbirds may eat fruits.

Deciduous tree. Zones 4-9. Notable for handsome winter pattern created by heavy trunk, heavy horizontal branches, and thick, deeply furrowed, corky bark. Leaves are 10 to 15 inches long with 5 to 13 glossy green leaflets; gives filtered shade. Leaves turn yellow in autumn but fall soon afterwards. Flowers are inconspicuous; male and female blooms are carried on separate trees. Fruit on female trees is black and pea-sized. Prefers deep, good garden soil. Established plants tolerate drought and high summer heat. Good lawn tree; roots are not at the surface and shade is not dense.

PHOTINIA

Clusters of red berries attract common flickers, robins, house finches, cedar waxwings, mockingbirds, variety of other birds.

Evergreen or deciduous shrubs or small trees. Grown for attractive foliage (especially new growth) and clusters of red berries. Susceptible to mildew, and often require a little pruning to control long, leggy shoots.

P. glabra. Japanese photinia. Evergreen. Zones 7-10. Broad, dense growth may reach 10 feet, sometimes more. Oval, 3-inch leaves are broadest toward the tip; coppery when young, scattered leaves turn red throughout the year. White flowers in 4-inch-wide clusters produce berries in late spring to early summer that are red at first, ripening to black.

P. serrulata. Chinese photinia. Evergreen. Zones 7-9. Very vigorous; can become tree sized — broad and dense to around 30 feet—but easily restricted to about 10 feet. New growth is bright copper, berries are red.

P. villosa. Oriental photinia. Deciduous. Zones 5-8. Fifteen-foot plant with about 10-foot spread. Oval leaves (3 inches long) start out pale gold with rosy tints, in autumn turn bright red before falling. Large red fruits appear in early fall, last into winter.

PICEA. SPRUCE

Year-round shelter; spring nesting sites. Often feeding on seeds in spring and fall are chickadees, American goldfinches, pine and evening grosbeaks, pine siskins, white-throated sparrows, red-breasted nuthatches. Fond of P. glauca are purple finches, evening grosbeaks, pine siskins, downy and hairy woodpeckers.

Evergreen trees. All of the following spruces are large trees, over 100 feet tall at maturity. Throughout their life are cone shaped or pyramidal. Quite trim in youth but tend to become sparse with age; at same time they also lose their lower branches.

P. abies. Norway spruce. Zones 3-9. Fast growing, deep green color, pyramid shaped. Branches grow horizontally; as plant ages, branchlets droop gracefully. Its 4 to 6-inch cones are largest among spruces.

P. engelmannii. Engelmann spruce. Zones 3-9. Native of Canada and states west of Rocky Mountains. Forms dense, light blue-green cone.

P. glauca. White spruce. Zones 3-9. Grows only to about 70 feet in cultivation, forming dense cone of pendulous twigs with silver green needles. Best in very cold-winter climates. Subspecies *P. g. densata* (Black Hills spruce) is slow growing, compact pyramid to about 20 feet in 35 years. Needles are bright blue-green.

P. pungens. Colorado spruce. Zones 3-9. Very stiff, regular, horizontal branches form broad pyramid; grows eventually to 100 feet. Color varies among seedling trees from dark green through all shades of blue-green to steely blue.

P. sitchensis. Sitka spruce. Zones 7-9. Tall and wide-spreading pyramid of bright green and silvery white needles. Native to Pacific Coast, but only happy in regions where there is plenty of cool, summer moisture.

PINUS. PINE

All-round value to variety of birds, providing shelter, food, nesting sites. Most commonly associated with pine are chickadees, brown creepers, blue jays, scrub and Steller's jays, Townsend's solitaires, evening and pine grosbeaks, nuthatches, pine siskins, hermit and pine warblers, many species of woodpeckers, kinglets, rufous-sided towhees. Magnolia warblers, purple finches frequently use P. strobus as nesting sites. Lovers of pine nuts include pine siskins, cardinals, chickadees, mourning doves, dark-eyed juncos, tufted titmice.

Evergreen trees. Most familiar needle-leafed evergreen. Numerous species range from timberline types to seashore inhabitants, can be selected to grow well in every zone. Generally speaking, pines grow best in full sun; soil need not be rich but should be well drained. If you are planting mainly for birds, choose the most dense species. The following list is far from complete but does contain some of the most useful pines, considering both birds and gardeners.

P. bungeana. Lacebark pine. Zones 5-9. Slow grower; eventually reaches 75 feet, often with several trunks. Shape is pyramidal to rounded. Smooth, dull gray bark flakes off to show smooth, creamy white branches and trunk. Tolerates hot summers.

P. canariensis. Canary Island pine. Zones 8-10. Fast grower to about 80 feet. Forms good, dense, narrow pyramid while young; becomes slender, but rounded, with age. Needles measure up to 1 foot; are blue-green to dark green.

P. cembra. Swiss stone pine. Zones 3-9. Although it may reach mature height of about 70 feet, growth is so slow that plants are best considered as shrubs. Spreading, short branches form narrow, dense pyramid. Overall neat appearance plus slow growth make it good plant for small gardens.

P. contorta. Shore or Beach pine. Zones 7-10. Growth is rapid but only to about 35 feet. One of best pines for small gardens; has dense foliage, is compact and generally pyramid shaped. Not at best in hot, dry areas.

P. c. latifolia. Lodgepole pine. Zones 6-10. Taller form (to 80 feet) of preceding species, but good for small gardens because it grows slowly. More irregular and open branched than *P. contorta*. Planted close together, grows tall and slim trunked, but planted singly is more heavy trunked and dense, although still slim. Not happy where summers are hot and dry.

P. flexilis. Limber pines. Zones 3-9. Slow growing, slender pyramid for many years. Suited to small gardens. Fairly dense, with short, fine-textured needles.

P. monticola. Western white pine. Zones 6-9. In contrast to *P. strobus,* is narrower, more symmetrical, and shorter (60 to 90 feet) at maturity. Growth is fast in first years, then slows down considerably. Fine and soft needles are blue-green, banded white beneath. Susceptible to white pine blister rust throughout Northwest and northern California.

P. nigra. Austrian black pine. Zones 5-9. Dense, stout pyramid, regularly formed with very stiff needles about 6 inches long. Equally good as specimen plant or massed in groups for windbreak.

P. radiata. Monterey pine. Zones 7-10. Too large for average gardens, but valuable for attractive shape (conical when young, rounded at maturity), good density, and very fast growth (as much as 50 feet in 12 years).

P. resinosa. Red or Norway pine. Zones 3-9. Broad, dark green pyramid with soft, flexible needles; good looking at all ages. Moderate grower to medium height of around 70 feet.

P. strobus. Eastern white pine. Zones 4-9. Most widely planted pine in eastern states. Needles are soft bluegreen, fine textured; present soft, graceful effect. Slender, dense pyramid in youth; becomes broader and more irregular with age. Eventually may reach 100 feet or more. Growth fairly slow during youthful years.

PLATANUS. SYCAMORE, PLANE TREE

Widely used as nesting sites by common flickers, orioles, acorn woodpeckers. Nests abandoned by woodpeckers often occupied by screech owls, chickadees, titmice, tree swallows. Hummingbirds use leaf fuzz for nests. Insects in spring are food for warblers and orioles. Tiny, ball-shaped fruits provide seeds which are eaten by purple and house finches, goldfinches, pine siskins, chickadees, grosbeaks, orioles, waxwings.

Deciduous trees. Large, rather massive trees with lobed, maplelike leaves. Bark is particularly attractive; older bark sheds in patches to reveal pale, smooth new bark beneath. Brown, ball-like seed clusters on long stalks hang from branches through winter. Foliage turns dusty brown in autumn.

P. acerifolia. London plane tree. Zones 6-10. Fast grower; reaches up to 80 feet with strong, straight trunk. Upper trunk and limbs are cream colored. Tolerates most soils; withstands smog, soot, dust, and reflected heat. Most resistant of sycamores to anthracnose disease but is least picturesque.

P. occidentalis. American sycamore, Buttonwood. Zones 5-10. Similar to *P. acerifolia,* but new bark is

Pine cones *not only provide seeds but also harbor various insects sought by this white-breasted nuthatch.*

whiter, tree is leafless longer, and seed balls appear singly on stems instead of in clusters. Occasionally grows with multiple or leaning trunks.

P. orientalis. Oriental plane tree. Zones 7-10. Habit is open and round headed, often growing as multiple-trunked specimen. More resistant to anthracnose disease than *P. occidentalis* and *P. racemosa.*

P. racemosa. California sycamore. Zones 7-10. Often grows as multi-trunked specimen or with artfully leaning trunk. Most irregular and picturesque of sycamores. Growth is rapid with ultimate height of 50 to 100 feet or more, depending upon how vertical or leaning the trunk is.

POINCIANA

Yellow and red summer flowers favored by several hummingbirds and some warblers.

Deciduous and evergreen shrub and tree. Quick and easy growth in hot sun with light, well-drained soil and deep but infrequent watering.

P. gilliesii. Bird of paradise bush. Evergreen shrub to small tree. Zones 8-10. Finely cut, filmy foliage on rather open, angular branch structure. Loses leaves in cold winters. Clustered yellow flowers have long (4 to 5-inch), protruding red stamens.

P. pulcherrima. Barbados pride, Dwarf poinciana. Deciduous shrub. Zones 9-10. Fast and dense to 10 feet high and wide. Leaves are composed of many dark green, ¾-inch leaflets. Clustered flowers are orange or red with long, red stamens.

PROSOPIS glandulosa torreyana. MESQUITE

Dense thicketlike growth provides nesting sites for number of desert birds. Seeds eaten by bobwhites, quail, doves.

Deciduous tree. Zones 8-9. Desert shade tree to 30 feet high and 40 feet wide or more. Crown is thicketlike canopy of branches and tiny bright green leaflets. Untrained, usually has several trunks from ground level. Best in deep soil where taproot will go down great distances for water. Tolerates drought, alkaline soil, or irrigated lawns. Survives in shallow, rocky soil, but will be shrubby.

PRUNUS. CHERRY, PLUM

Attract variety of birds: bobwhites, blue jays, robins, red-headed woodpeckers, common flickers, grosbeaks (rose-breasted, evening, and pine), brown thrashers, sparrows, starlings, cedar waxwings, Swainson's thrushes, eastern kingbirds, gray catbirds, house finches. Interested in fruits of P. pensylvanica and P. serotina are eastern bluebirds, common flickers, grosbeaks (evening, rose-breasted, and black-headed), cardinals, gray catbirds, kingbirds, mockingbirds, northern orioles, robins, brown thrashers, cedar waxwings, red-headed woodpeckers. Insects bring flycatchers.

Mostly deciduous trees and shrubs. Vast number of plants: apricots, almonds, peaches, nectarines, plums, and cherries. Most attractive to birds are *P. pensylvanica* and *P. serotina*. Many native species are not often planted because leaves can poison livestock or because plants are short lived. But because their fruits are summer delicacies to birds, they are worth considering for the rural or "wild" gardens. Actually, any cherry will attract birds when in fruit, but the trees in the following selection will have little or no human competition for fruit.

P. americana. Wild plum. Zones 4-8. Yellow-fruited tree (about 20 feet tall) with white flowers. Leaves are willowlike, narrow, and 3 to 4 inches long. Native to eastern states.

P. besseyi. Western sand cherry. Shrub. Zones 3-8. Native to midwestern United States and Canada. Seven-foot plant producing small, black cherries in fall. A selected form, Hansen's bush cherry, has larger and more abundant fruit. Either has excellent fruits for eating or cooking.

P. maackii. Amur chokecherry. Zones 3-9. One of the taller cherries (40 to 50 feet) and round headed. Attractive golden brown bark peels off in strips. White flowers are followed by small black fruits.

P. mahaleb. Mahaleb cherry. Zones 6-9. Open tree to 30 feet with small, oval leaves; clusters of small black fruits follow fragrant white blossoms. Frequently used as understock onto which commercial cherries are grafted.

P. maritima. Beach plum. Shrub. Zones 4-8. Favorite New England seashore native, known for its delicious 1-inch purple fruit. Dense, rounded bush to about 6 feet tall. Several named varieties (selected for superior fruit) are sold.

P. nigra. Canada or Red plum. Zones 3-9. Upright, rather narrow tree that may reach 30 feet; leaves are 3 to 5 inches long. White flowers fade to pink; resulting plums are egg shaped, red (sometimes blushed yellow), and up to 1½ inches long.

P. padus. European bird cherry. Zones 4-9. Another fairly tall cherry; may reach 40 feet with somewhat open crown. White, fragrant flowers are carried in narrow, drooping clusters; small fruit is black. Leaves (3 to 5 inches long) appear quite early in spring.

P. pensylvanica. Wild red or Pin cherry. Tree. Zones 3-9. Distinctly short-lived but excellent for naturalistic or woodland gardens which approximate natural habitat at or in forest's edge. Height is about 30 feet but habit frequently is shrubby. Attractive plant throughout the year: white flowers in spring, small red fruit in summer, red autumn color, and glossy red bark for winter interest.

P. pumila. Sand cherry. Shrub. Zones 3-8. Native to shores of the Great Lakes where it grows up to 6 feet. Fruit is small and black-purple.

P. serotina. Black cherry. Zones 4-9. Largest of cherries at mature height of 90 feet. Best known for use in making furniture. Dense crown consists of 5-inch, narrow, and shiny leaves carried on somewhat drooping branches. Hanging clusters of white flowers are followed by small red cherries that turn black.

P. tomentosa. Nanking or Manchu cherry. Shrub. Zones 3-8. Probably the most ornamental of shrubby *Prunus* species. Useful as specimen plant or as attractive hedge. Bright red, ½-inch cherries appear in early summer.

PYRACANTHA. FIRETHORN

Striking masses of reddish fruit draw most fruit eaters: bluebirds, mockingbirds, brown thrashers, cedar waxwings, quail, fox sparrows, cardinals, curve-billed thrashers, house finches. Robins are especially fond of berries; they often gorge on a fermenting late crop, inducing a mild state of intoxication.

Evergreen shrubs. Ease of growth and versatility in landscaping use are two prime reasons for the popularity of these shrubs. Foliage is small but always good looking. Masses of tiny white flowers create a good display in their season, are followed by brilliant red to orange berries in tightly packed clusters. Several species and many named varieties are sold: big, sprawling shrubs; well-behaved large bushes; limber sorts that can be trained against fences or walls; and low, spreading types suitable for foreground or even ground cover plantings. Plants need full sun and grow best where soil is not constantly wet. Fireblight is their worst enemy; see under *Crataegus* on page 64 for control measures. The following species and varieties provide a sampling of those you may find for sale.

P. atalantioides. Gibbs firethorn. Zones 7-10. A 15 to 18-foot shrub with fruit that appears in fall and hangs on into winter.

P. coccinea. Scarlet firethorn. Zones 6-10. An 8 to 10-foot, rounded plant bearing orange-red berries in autumn. Several varieties have been selected and named, of which 'Lalandel' and 'Kasan' are the most cold tolerant.

P. fortuneana. Chinese firethorn. Zones 7-10. Spreading growth to 15 feet high and 10 feet wide with limber branches make it well adapted to training against a vertical surface. Variety 'Graberi' has huge clusters of dark red fruits lasting from midautumn through winter; its growth is more upright.

P. koidzumii. Formosa firethorn. Zones 8-10. Bulky, upright shrub to 10 feet tall and nearly as wide, bearing large clusters of big, scarlet fruits.

Low growing pyracanthas include the following varieties: 'Santa Cruz', 'Tiny Tim', and 'Walderi'.

Pyracantha (Firethorn) has large, showy clusters of berries; colors are red, orange, or yellow.

PYRUS. PEAR

Fruit favored by gray catbirds, purple finches, house finches, northern orioles, robins, mockingbirds, sparrows, blue and scrub jays, common flickers, cedar waxwings.

Deciduous trees. Zones 5-9, but adaptability varies according to variety. Long-lived, pyramidal trees with vertical branching, 30 to 40 feet tall. Clusters of white flowers in early spring precede glossy, bright green, oval leaves. More tolerant of damp, heavy soil than most other fruit trees. Dieback caused by fireblight can be a problem, but degree of resistance varies according to variety. Cut out blighted branches well below dead part; wash pruning tools with disinfectant between each cut.

QUERCUS. OAK

Good food, shelter, and nesting tree. Acorns gathered by woodpeckers, chickadees, evening grosbeaks, plain and tufted titmice, towhees, all the jays, horned larks, California quail, white-breasted nuthatches. Visiting specific oak species for insects are the following: Q. coccinea — blue jays; Q. laurifolia — blue jays, common woodpeckers; Q. marilandica — blue jays; Q. nigra — bobwhites, blue jays, brown thrashers, tufted titmice, several species of woodpeckers; Q. phellos — bobwhites, blue jays, tufted titmice.

Deciduous or evergreen trees. If your property is large, there's hardly an oak you couldn't consider planting, being restricted only by varying hardiness among species. But because the majority of oaks are large to massive trees, choices for small gardens are limited. The species described below are smaller oaks, most of which usually mature at 60 feet or less.

Q. agrifolia. Coast live oak. Evergreen. Zones 9-10. Dense, round-headed California native adaptable to normal garden conditions if planted as young seedling, acorn, or nursery stock. Some variation in leaf size and shape and in tree habit, but normally foliage is dark green, hollylike, and 1 to 3 inches long. Young trees grow quickly with regular watering.

Q. bicolor. Swamp white oak. Deciduous. Zones 4-9. Grows to 60 feet or less. Round headed and not too spreading. Grows well in moist soils. Dark green, lobed leaves may be up to 6 inches long, are white underneath. Autumn color is bronzy yellow to red.

Q. chrysolepis. Canyon live oak. Evergreen. Zones 8-10. Round headed or somewhat spreading tree to 20 to 60 feet high. Oval 1 to 2-inch-long leaves are shiny, medium green above, grayish or whitish beneath; smooth or toothed edges. Bark is smooth and gray-white.

(Continued on next page)

Q. coccinea. Scarlet oak. Deciduous. Zones 5-10. Native to the eastern third of states. Growth is moderate to rapid in good, deep soil where it ultimately reaches 60 to 80 feet. Unlike most other oaks, has open rather than dense crown; deep roots make it good tree to garden or grow lawn under. Glossy green, lobed leaves turn brilliant scarlet in autumn wherever nights are nippy, not as bright in warm-autumn regions.

Q. garryana. Oregon white oak. Deciduous. Zones 7-9. Broad, round-headed growth reaches 40 to 90 feet, often with picturesquely twisted branches. Trunk is grayish, ruggedly checked. Lobed leaves (to 6 inches long) are dark glossy green above, rusty or downy beneath. Casts moderate shade; has deep root system.

Q. ilex. Holly or Holm oak. Evergreen. Zones 9-10. Height and spread are about equal (40 to 70 feet). Leaves vary in shape and size to 3 inches long and nearly half as wide, either toothed (like some hollies) or smooth edged; color is rich green above, yellowish or silvery below. Tolerates wind and salt air, although tends to be shrubby where exposed to constant sea wind. Growth is moderately rapid in good soil with ample water. Gives dense shade.

Q. laurifolia. Laurel oak. Semi-evergreen. Zones 7-10. Native to southeastern states. Dense, round-headed tree 40 to 60 feet tall. Leaves are shining dark green, 4 to 6 inches long and rather oval, usually without lobes.

Q. marilandica. Blackjack oak. Deciduous. Zones 7-9. Slow-growing, small tree particularly adapted to poor, dry soils. Habit is irregular to 30 feet or so, but often shrubby for many years. Attractive, glossy, slightly lobed leaves turn yellow or brown in fall.

Q. nigra. Water oak. Deciduous to semi-evergreen. Zones 7-10. Fairly slender and fine-textured oak from southeastern states. Blue-green, 3-inch leaves have few or no lobes. May reach 75 feet; adapts to moist or wet soils.

Q. palustris. Pin oak. Deciduous. Zones 5-10. Moderate to fairly rapid growth to 50 to 80 feet with distinctive branching habit. Broadly pyramidal with three types of limbs: upright toward top, horizontal in the middle, and pointing downward in lowest section. If you cut lowest branches to make tree you can walk under, branches above cuts will become pendulous and grow to ground. Simplest solution is to allow tree to grow as huge shrub branching from ground up. Glossy green leaves are deeply lobed, turn yellow to red and finally to brown in autumn; many hang on throughout winter. Needs ample water and good drainage; will develop chlorosis in alkaline soils.

Q. phellos. Willow oak. Deciduous. Zones 6-9. Most delicate of all oaks in foliage pattern. Leaves are up to 5 inches long but no more than 1 inch wide and smooth edged — much like willow leaves. Grows to 50 feet or more with a branching habit much like Q. palustris. Fall color is yellow.

Q. rubra. Red oak. Deciduous. Zones 4-10. Fastest grower among oaks (to around 75 feet). Pyramidal when young, round headed at maturity. Leaves are lobed, 5 to 8 inches long, 3 to 5 inches wide; new

leaves are red in spring and turn to dark red, ruddy brown, or orange in fall. High-branching habit, reasonably open shade, and deep roots make it good tree to garden under. Needs good soil and ample water.

Q. suber. Cork oak. Evergreen. Zones 8-10. Moderate growth rate to 70 feet high and wide with distinctive thick, fissured, corky trunk and large branches. Source of commercial cork. Trunk and limb structure massive; foliage fine textured. Established trees tolerate drought.

RHAMNUS. BUCKTHORN

Occasionally seen eating fruits: scrub jays, mockingbirds, Swainson's thrushes, California thrashers, robins, California quail, wrentits, yellow-bellied sapsuckers, fox sparrows, purple finches, waxwings, brown towhees. Plant has insects and spiders year-round.

Evergreen and deciduous shrubs or small trees. Neither especially attractive nor unattractive ornamentals — just rather indifferent in landscape effect. Best use is in a "wild" garden or in an inconspicuous spot in the yard.

R. alaternus. Italian buckthorn. Evergreen shrub. Zones 7-10. Fast, dense, and large shrub to 20 feet that also will double as small tree. Oval, bright shiny green leaves up to 2 inches long. Following inconspicuous flowers, fruit is black. Takes drought or regular watering, heat, wind, sun or part shade, and shearing.

R. californica. Coffeeberry. Evergreen shrub. Zones 7-10. Growth varies from low spreading to upright, 3 to 15 feet. Leaves are 1 to 3 inches long, shining to dull dark green. Large berries begin green, turn red, then finally black.

R. caroliniana. Indian cherry or Yellow bush. Deciduous. Zones 6-9. Large shrub or small tree to about 25 feet. Oblong leaves (4 to 6 inches) are larger than most other species. Small fruits are red for a while but eventually turn black.

R. cathartica. Common buckthorn. Deciduous shrub. Zones 3-8. Upright and irregular growth habit to about 12 feet, yet can be trained as informal hedge. Branches are somewhat spiny. Male and female flowers borne on separate plants; both are necessary for female plants to bear black fruit. Leaves are oval and dark green, to 3 inches long, with finely toothed margins.

R. frangula. Alder buckthorn. Deciduous shrub or small tree. Zones 3-9. Upright growth to 15 feet, spreading out as plant gets older. Rather round, 3-inch, glossy dark green leaves are backdrop for red and black fruits. Autumn foliage is bright yellow.

R. purshiana. Cascara sagrada. Deciduous shrub or small tree. Zones 4-9. Usually a tall shrub but sometimes may become 20 to 30-foot tree. Prominently veined, elliptical leaves are dark green, up to 8 inches long and 2 inches wide. Fruit is black. Autumn foliage turns yellow, then drops, revealing attractive branching pattern. Grows in dense shade or in full sun with ample water.

RHUS. SUMAC

Winter fruit supplements diet of many birds. Attracted to specific species are the following: gray catbirds, eastern bluebirds, cardinals, robins, starlings, mockingbirds, hermit thrushes—R. copallina; eastern bluebirds, mockingbirds, gray catbirds, wood thrushes—R. glabra; golden-crowned sparrows, yellow-rumped warblers, goldfinches, thrashers, mockingbirds, California quail, evening grosbeaks — R. integrifolia, R. laurina, R. ovata; gray catbirds, eastern bluebirds, black-capped chickadees, evening and pine grosbeaks, robins, brown towhees, starlings, hermit thrushes—R. typhina; bushtits, flycatchers, towhees, white-crowned sparrows are visitors to southwestern species. Bushes provide good shelter.

Deciduous and evergreen shrubs or small trees. Of the ornamental sumacs, the deciduous types are the most cold tolerant (some extremely so) and thrive in poor soil, though they need some water to grow well. They tend to produce suckers, especially if their roots are disturbed by soil cultivation. Evergreen sumacs will grow in almost any soil but it must be well drained; soggy soils may be fatal.

R. aromatica. Fragrant sumac. Deciduous. Zones 6-9. Spreading by underground suckers, this short sumac (about 3 feet high) makes a good bank cover for dry slopes or a foreground plant for taller shrubs. Dense, hairy leaves consist of three oval leaflets, each about 3 inches long and broadly toothed; leaves turn yellow to bright red in autumn. Hairy, berrylike, red fruits ripen in summer.

R. copallina. Shining sumac. Deciduous. Zones 5-9. Treelike to about 30 feet in warmer zones but shrubby to only about 10 feet in colder areas. The many leaflets (4 to 5 inches long) are glossy dark green, becoming brilliant scarlet in fall. Red fruits ripen in fall, but both male and female plants are needed for their production.

R. glabra. Smooth sumac. Deciduous. Zones 3-9. Rangy, spreading (by underground suckers) 10-foot shrub to 20-foot small tree. Many 2 to 5-inch-long leaflets per leaf are deep green above, whitish beneath, and turn brilliant scarlet in fall. An additional showy autumn display is red fruits in conical clusters, lasting into winter after leaves have fallen. Both male and female plants are necessary to produce fruits.

R. integrifolia. Lemonade berry. Evergreen. Zones 9-10. Usually a rounded shrub to around 10 feet high and wide. Leathery, dark green leaves (to 2½ inches long) are oval to round. Inconspicuous flowers are followed by clusters of small red fruits in summer. Native to coastal southern California and grows best there. Objects to intense, dry summer heat. A similar plant for

inland areas is R. ovata. Can even be trained as hedge or espalier against fence or wall.

R. laurina. Laurel sumac. Evergreen shrub. Zones 9-10. Native to coastal southern California. Grows best where frost is rare. Rapid growth gives a 6 to 15-foot, round-topped shrub with reddish branchlets. Light green leaves are oval, 2 to 4 inches long, often with pink margins and leaf stalks. White, berrylike fruits follow inconspicuous flowers that appear in spring and often continue throughout the year.

R. ovata. Sugar bush. Evergreen shrub. Zones 8-10. Similar to R. integrifolia with only minor leaf differences. Succeeds in hot, inland areas where R. integrifolia won't, but will not do well along the coast where it might be subject to salt spray.

R. typhina. Staghorn sumac. Deciduous shrub or small tree. Zones 3-9. Similar to R. glabra but can grow about 10 feet taller, and the current year's new branches are covered with fuzz similar to that found on newly formed deer antlers. Striking in autumn when growing in large clumps.

RIBES. CURRANT

Early blossoms attract resident and migrating hummingbirds. Other birds feeding on blue-black berries (and sometimes blossoms) include robins, thrashers, waxwings, thrushes, gray catbirds, eastern bluebirds, jays, solitaires, towhees, common flickers, chickadees, finches, fox sparrows.

Deciduous or evergreen shrubs. Plants without spines are called currants; those with spines are gooseberries.

(Continued on next page)

Ribes sanguineum *(Red flowering currant) flowers attract hummingbirds, fruits attract other birds.*

R. aureum. Golden currant. Deciduous. Zones 4-10. Erect to 6 feet tall, with light green, lobed and toothed leaves. Clusters of bright yellow flowers (to 2½ inches long) in spring; summer berries are yellow to red to black.

R. sanguineum. Red flowering currant. Deciduous. Zones 6-10. Maplelike leaves (to 2½ inches wide) clothe a 4 to 12-foot shrub. Deep pink to red small flowers in 2 to 4-inch drooping clusters are produced throughout spring; blue-black berries follow.

R. speciosum. Fuchsia-flowering gooseberry. Nearly evergreen. Zones 8-10. Erect, 3 to 6 feet tall with spiny, often bristly stems. One-inch leaves are thick and dark green. Deep red, drooping flowers in late winter to early spring are followed by gummy, bristly berries. Several plants make good barrier.

ROSA. ROSE

Excellent nesting sites. Provides food throughout winter. Eating rose hips or fruits of various species are cardinals, bobwhites, wood thrushes, robins. Returning to R. multiflora are mockingbirds, cedar waxwings, song sparrows, eastern bluebirds, cardinals, American goldfinches, grosbeaks. Other birds eating rose hips or fruits may be Townsend's solitaires, Swainson's thrushes, vireos, California quail, chickadees.

Deciduous shrubs (or semi-evergreen in warm climates). The more aggressive rose species can serve either or both of two purposes for birds. If their fruits (called "hips") are small (roughly ½-inch diameter or less), they provide food. If growth habit is dense and thicket-forming, the plants furnish excellent protective cover and nesting sites. The four species described here fulfill all these requirements. Their flowers are attractive in mass, although they should not be compared individually to modern garden hybrids.

R. carolina. Carolina rose. Zones 5-10. Suckering growth habit produces dense thickets about 3 feet high. Single, 2-inch pink flowers come in spring and are followed in early fall by small red hips.

R. multiflora. Japanese or Multiflora rose. Zones 6-10. Large, spreading shrub best for a good-sized "wild" garden or as a hedgerow on rural property. Arching, dense growth produces plant about 10 feet tall and wide. Inch-wide, single white flowers appear in large clusters in spring, resulting in great numbers of red hips in autumn. Thornless forms of this rose are used mainly for understock on which to bud modern hybrids, but are less useful than thorny types for keeping out bird predators.

R. rugosa. Ramanas rose, Sea tomato. Zones 3-10. The red hips of this species (and its numerous named varieties) may be a little large for most birds, but the plant is unexcelled for attractiveness plus durability. Dense growth from 3 to 8 feet tall is clothed in handsome glossy green, heavily veined foliage. Flowers are

3 to 4 inches across and (depending upon the variety) single to double, and white, pink, purplish red, or creamy yellow; long blooming season. Takes hard freezes, wind, drought, and salt spray in stride. In cold climates autumn foliage is orange to red.

R. virginiana. Virginia rose. Zones 4-10. May be thought of as larger version of *R. carolina*, spreading by suckers into dense, upright thickets to 6 feet tall. You can keep it shorter by trimming or by periodic cutting to the ground. Foliage is bright glossy green, turning to red and orange in fall. Single, pink, 2 to 3-inch blooms appear in spring or early summer, followed by small red fruits in autumn.

ROSMARINUS officinalis. ROSEMARY

Towhees seek good nesting sites; hummingbirds like flower nectar. Used for shelter during winter by white and golden-crowned sparrows. Goldfinches, quail, towhees also frequent visitors.

Evergreen. Zones 7-10. Shrub (3 to 6 feet high) with somewhat variable growth habit, generally spreading as wide or wider than high. Very narrow (nearly needlelike), inch-long leaves are glossy dark green above, grayish white beneath. Clusters of small lavender-blue blossoms (each later producing a tiny seed) appear in winter or early spring. Extremely rugged, trouble-free plants, requiring occasional summer water only in hottest regions once plants are established. Grows best in poor, rocky, well-drained soil — too much water and rich soil produces rank growth leading to a woody, more sparse plant. Wet, heavy soil is fatal. Variety 'Prostratus' grows about 2 feet tall and spreads widely; its branches curve and twist gracefully. Variety 'Tuscan Blue' is rigidly upright to 6 feet with broader leaves and blue-violet blossoms. Variety 'Lockwood de Forest' resembles 'Prostratus' but has bluer flowers, while variety 'Collingwood Ingram' has intense violet-blue flowers on plant somewhat shorter and more spreading than the species.

SALIX. WILLOW

Wide variety of birds, including bushtits, warblers, vireos, chickadees, and some flycatchers may visit willows for aphids, caterpillars, other insects. Buds are eaten by evening and pine grosbeaks, goldfinches; hummingbirds and bushtits are often seen collecting seed cotton for nests. Usually good nesting locations for vireos, warblers, goldfinches, grosbeaks, acorn woodpeckers, bushtits.

Deciduous trees. Although willows will grow in a wide variety of climates, best performance is where there are pronounced winters. Very fast growing. Takes any soil;

most tolerate poor drainage. All have invasive roots, need plenty of water, and are hard to garden under.

S. alba. White willow. Zones 3-10. Upright and open grow to 75 feet. Several varieties are sold: 'Chermisina', with red young branches; *sericea*, with gray-green leaves; 'Tristis' (the Golden weeping willow), with yellowish twigs and foliage and weeping growth; and 'Vitellina' (Yellowstem willow) with yellow twigs and upright growth.

S. babylonica. Weeping willow. Zones 6-10. Grows 30 to 50 feet high with equal or greater spread. Leaves are long (3 to 6 inches) and narrow on drooping branches. Attractive grown alongside pond or stream.

S. blanda. Wisconsin weeping willow. Zones 5-10. Similar to *S. babylonica* but may grow slightly larger, is less weeping, and has broader, more blue-green leaves.

S. discolor. Pussy willow. Zones 3-10. Upright and sometimes shrubby to about 20 feet, with slender red-brown stems and oval green leaves (2 to 4 inches long) that are lighter and bluish underneath. Gray, furry catkins appear in early spring before leaves.

S. matsudana. Hankow willow. Zones 4-10. Upright, pyramidal growth to 40 or 50 feet. Leaves are narrow, bright green, 2 to 4 inches long. Can thrive on less water than most other willows.

SAMBUCUS. ELDERBERRY

Blue and red elderberries favorite food of many birds. Particularly partial to berries are black-headed, rose-breasted, and evening grosbeaks; blue jays and scrub jays; cardinals; song sparrows; vireos; mockingbirds; northern orioles; robins; flickers; gray catbirds; white-throated sparrows; cedar waxwings; towhees; hermit thrushes; wrentits; white-breasted nuthatches; titmice; brown thrashers; bluebirds; doves; finches; quail; downy woodpeckers. Marks of yellow-bellied sapsuckers frequently found on bark. Nesting sites for vireos, goldfinches, grosbeaks, mockingbirds, warblers.

Deciduous shrubs or trees. Tree species are vigorous but shrublike, usually too coarse and rangy for foreground planting. Excellent in "wild" garden or placed in spot not too prominent. Can be kept dense and shrubby by severe pruning every dormant season. Shrub species have the same uses and limitations but are naturally shorter plants. Whenever they become overgrown, cut to the ground; they will grow again from the roots. All elderberries prefer moist soil but are drought tolerant. Fruit ripens in summer.

S. caerulea. Blue elderberry. Zones 6-9. Shrub or spreading tree to 50 feet. Leaves are 5 to 8 inches long, divided into five to nine leaflets each up to 6 inches long. Flat-topped clusters of creamy white flowers are followed by blue-black, round berries.

S. canadensis. American elder. Zones 4-8. Ten-foot shrub with leaves consisting of about seven leaflets, each up to 5 inches long. Large, flat-topped clusters of white flowers produce black summer berries. Several varieties are sold, varying in leaf color or type, color of berries, or size of flower clusters.

S. mexicana. Zones 7-8. Generally similar to *S. caerulea*, but leaflets are fewer and smaller, flower clusters and berries are smaller and less juicy.

S. pubens. Scarlet elder. Shrub. Zones 5-8. Similar leaves to *S. canadensis*, but creamy white flowers are carried in pyramidal clusters. Summer berries are red.

S. racemosa. Red elder. Shrub. Zones 5-7. Smaller plant (6 to 10 feet) than the other species listed here with correspondingly smaller leaves. Creamy white flowers are in small dome-shaped clusters, followed by bright red berries in summer.

SASSAFRAS albidum. SASSAFRAS

Berries enjoyed by eastern bluebirds, bobwhites, gray catbirds, robins, red-eyed vireos.

Deciduous tree. Zones 5-9. Rapid growth to about 25 feet, then slows down to eventual 60-foot, pyramidal tree. Trunk is heavy, branches rather short. Leaves are quite variable in shape — oval, lobed on one side, or lobed on both sides; they turn orange and scarlet in autumn. Small blue-black berries come in early fall but ability of single tree to bear fruit is unpredictable: some produce only male flowers, some only female flowers, some produce both on same tree or have both sexes combined in single flower. Best in sandy, well-drained, non-alkaline soil. Not drought tolerant.

SCHINUS. PEPPER TREE

Berry eaters like small, peppercornlike berries. In fall and winter, ripened berries on female pepper tree are favorite food of mockingbirds, cedar waxwings, robins, hermit thrushes. In southwestern regions, flickers, jays, and thrashers feed on berries. Yellow-bellied sapsuckers frequently seek the sap. Long, drooping branchlets and leaves make ideal places for long, socklike nests of bushtits.

Evergreen trees. Two distinctly different appearing trees come from South America; both have small round berries resembling peppercorns.

S. molle. California pepper tree. Zones 9-10. Graceful like weeping willow (*Salix babylonica*) with attraction of heavy, gnarled and twisted trunk on older specimens. Mature trees are rounded to 40 feet high and wide. Bright green leaves are divided into many narrow, 1½ to 2-inch-long leaflets on pendant branchlets that sweep the ground unless trimmed up. Hanging clusters of rose-colored berries come in fall and winter. Will grow in any soil; tolerates drought (when established) and poor drainage. Possible drawbacks are constant litter from falling leaflets and ripening fruits (in season), and greedy surface roots than can crack paving and foundations, or clog sewers and drains.

S. terebinthifolius. Brazilian pepper. Zones 9-10. Moderate growth rate produces umbrella-shaped 30-foot tree with equal spread; can grow as multi-trunked specimen. Compared to *S. molle*, does not have pendant branches but does have darker green, glossy leaves with fewer but larger leaflets. Surface roots can be discouraged by deep, infrequent watering and little fertilizer.

SHEPHERDIA. Buffalo berry

Good berry producer; attracts pine grosbeaks, gray catbirds, hermit thrushes, brown thrashers, hairy and red-headed woodpeckers, Swainson's thrushes, common flickers, red-eyed towhees.

Deciduous shrubs. Valuable in areas where great stress is put on plants by these elements: poor, dry soil; wind; extremely cold winters. Bear fruit only when male and female plants are grown together.

S. argentea. Silverleaf or Buffaloberry. Zones 3-8. Called by first common name because of silvery leaves (both sides) and branches. Leaves are oblong (to about 2½ inches long) on a thorny shrub or small tree (as high as 18 feet). Small, egg-shaped fruit is yellow to red, ripening in late summer to early fall. Blooms are inconspicuous. Good hedge plant.

S. canadensis. Russet buffaloberry. Zones 3-8. Smaller (only to about 8 feet), thornless shrub of relatively open growth. Leaves are similar, but silvery only on undersides.

SORBUS. Mountain ash

Produce clusters of reddish berries. Preferring the berries of S. americana are eastern bluebirds, gray catbirds, evening and pine grosbeaks, northern orioles, cedar waxwings, red-headed woodpeckers, Swainson's thrushes, robins, thrashers, flickers, purple finches, towhees, song sparrows, white-breasted nuthatches. Often seen feeding on berries of S. aucuparia are gray catbirds, pine grosbeaks, northern orioles, brown thrashers, robins, cedar waxwings, red-headed woodpeckers, starlings.

Deciduous trees. Flowers, fruit, and fall color provide changing interest in three or four seasons. Conspicuous, flat-topped clusters of white flowers in spring are

Sorbus aucuparia *(European mountain ash) has red-orange berries, tempting this red-shafted flicker.*

followed by equally showy berry clusters, varying in color among species.

S. alnifolia. Korean mountain ash. Zones 6-9. Rounded tree branched to the ground (if permitted); mature height about 60 feet. Distinctive among mountain ashes for rather oval, strongly ribbed leaves of about 6 inches long that are not broken into numerous leaflets. Autumn foliage color and berries are orange to red. Bark is gray and smooth.

S. americana. American mountain ash. Zones 3-9. Native to woodlands of Canada and United States from the east coast to the prairies. Thirty-foot tree with bright red berries. Leaves are bright green and long, composed of up to 15 leaflets. Needs acid soil.

S. aucuparia. European mountain ash. Zones 3-9. Most widely planted of mountain ashes. Fairly fast grower to 50 feet in oval to rounded form. Leaves are divided into 9 to 15 leaflets, each 1 to 2 inches long; are dull green above, gray-green below, and turn rusty yellow in fall. Fruits are red-orange. Requires sun, well-drained soil, and summer water.

S. decora. Showy mountain ash. Zones 3-8. Very similar to *S. americana*; has larger, showier fruits.

SYMPHORICARPOS. Snowberry

Laden with fruits throughout winter. Commonly seen looking for their share of food are waxwings, evening and pine grosbeaks, robins, hermit and Swainson's thrushes, towhees, 30 other species. In early spring, hummingbirds may visit flowers. In northwestern regions, fruits known as "survival food" for variety of birds, but not favored food.

Deciduous shrubs. Fairly low (none over 6 feet), rather airy shrubs whose main decorative feature is berrylike fruit hanging on after leaves fall. Many species spread by root suckers, making them good erosion control plants on sloping land, or suiting them for thicket or hedge planting. None are particular about soil type or amount of moisture once established.

S. albus. Common snowberry. Zones 3-10. Upright but with arching stems, growing from 2 to 6 feet tall. Leaves are rounded, dull green, and up to 2 inches long but may be up to 4 inches and lobed on new sucker growth. White, ½-inch fruits appear in late summer, continue into winter.

S. chenaultii. Chenault coral berry. Zones 5-10. A hybrid of *S. albus*, resembling it except for a shorter, more compact growth habit. Fruit is slightly larger, red on the side facing outward, white on the interior side; often spots of one color appear on the other.

S. orbiculatus. Coral berry or Indian currant. Zones 3-10. Resembles *S. albus* except for fruits, which are smaller, purplish red, and borne in clusters all along the branches.

THUJA. Arborvitae

Mainly used for shelter in dense foliage. Cone seeds are important to a few bird species. The cones found on T. occidentalis are liked by pine siskins, several species of thrushes, warblers. The cones of T. plicata feed Swainson's thrushes, mockingbirds, pine grosbeaks.

Evergreen trees or shrubs. Dense, neat, and symmetrical; carry foliage in flat sprays. Singly, arborvitaes are formal in effect; usually globular, conical, or cylindrical. Many selected forms are sold, most of which are shrub sized, rather than tree height. Some of the most widely sold varieties have foliage that is yellow-green or even bright golden yellow. Best performance always is in regions having moist air without much summer heat. In addition to intolerance of dryness and heat, all are sensitive to wind, dust, and the pollutants of city air.

T. occidentalis. American arborvitae. Tree. Zones 3-10. Upright to almost columnar with bright green to yellowish green leaf sprays. In severe cold foliage turns brown, reducing value in winter landscape. Sixty-foot tree in the wild, but actual species seldom is sold. Usually you find one of its varieties, most of which are much shorter. Taller varieties make good clipped or unclipped screens. Needs moist soil and moist atmosphere to perform best.

T. plicata. Western red cedar. Tree. Zones 6-10. In native western states, may exceed 200 feet; in gardens is much shorter pyramid which can be restricted by careful clipping. Graceful, lacy appearance comes from drooping branchlets that are closely set with dark green, scalelike leaves. Does not brown nearly as much in winter as does *T. occidentalis*.

TSUGA. Hemlock

Good shelter, food (cone seeds), nesting sites for pine siskins, mountain and black-capped chickadees, American goldfinches, blue jays, evening and pine grosbeaks, purple finches. Swainson's thrushes, robins also feed on the cone seeds; sometimes seek nesting sites.

Evergreen trees. Mostly very large trees with especially graceful foliage. Branches are horizontal to drooping with needlelike leaves flattened and narrowed at bases to form distinct, short stalks. Small, brown cones hang down from branches. Best growth in acid soil with ample moisture, high summer humidity, and protection from hot sun and wind; don't do well in cities.

T. canadensis. Canada hemlock. Zones 5-9. Native to eastern states and Canada; grows to 90-foot, dark green, pyramidal tree. In western states is much smaller, often tending to grow two or more trunks. Fine lawn tree or background planting; also can be clipped into outstandingly beautiful hedge.

T. caroliniana. Carolina hemlock. Zones 5-9. Generally identical to *T. canadensis*, but somewhat more tolerant of city atmosphere.

T. heterophylla. Western hemlock. Zones 6-9. Grows best in native region — cool, moist northwest areas west of Cascade Mountains. Growth is rapid to well over 100 feet, but can be easily trimmed as large hedge.

T. mertensiana. Mountain hemlock. Zones 6-9. Native to mountains from Alaska into California. More at home in native range, particularly where climate is cool and moist. Growing wild it reaches 50 to 90 feet, but in lowland gardens is much lower and rather slow growing. Foliage is silvery blue-green.

ULMUS. Elm

Abundance of papery seeds in spring. Enjoyed by pine siskins, house and purple finches, goldfinches. Other birds feeding on buds or fruits are evening and rose-breasted grosbeaks, cardinals, bobwhites, black-capped chickadees. Nesting sites coveted by northern orioles, vireos, yellow warblers, black-headed grosbeaks, blue jays.

Deciduous or partially evergreen trees. Wood of many species is weak and subject to splitting and breaking in storms; roots are close to the surface, making it difficult to grow other plants nearby. However, *U. americana* (American elm) has unique vase-shaped silhouette; is favorite nesting tree of Northern orioles. If you have one, enjoy and treasure it. But unless you have a very large or rural garden, planting one just for birds will not be as rewarding as will planting of other deciduous trees listed in this section.

VACCINIUM. BLUEBERRY

**Fleshy berries are favored by black-capped chicka-
dees, kingbirds, eastern bluebirds, pine grosbeaks,
rufous-sided and red-eyed towhees, robins, hermit
thrushes, orioles, tufted titmice, brown thrashers,
common flickers, 90 other bird species.**

Deciduous or evergreen. Graceful shrubs of various
sizes with attractive, edible fruits and colorful fall foliage in the deciduous species. All require acid soil —
but not necessarily good soil — and organic matter
such as peat moss or leaf mold.

V. corymbosum. Highbush blueberry. Deciduous.
Zones 4-9. Various varieties of commercial blueberries
have been selected from this species. Under favorable
conditions it will reach 12 feet tall, but usually is about
half that height. Bronze new growth becomes glossy
green, 3-inch oval leaves; in autumn leaves turn brilliant red or orange. Clusters of white or pinkish, urn-
shaped flowers develop into characteristic blue-black
berries that have a powdery gray "bloom" on them.
Berries ripen throughout summer. Plants grow well in
shade but are more compact when located in full sun.

V. ovatum. Evergreen huckleberry or Box blueberry.
Evergreen. Zones 7-9. Only 2 to 3 feet tall in sun, but
will go up to 10 feet in shade; best development is in
semi-shade. Young plants are spreading but become
taller than wide, and compact as they grow older.
Bronzy new growth matures into ½ to 1¼-inch, lustrous, dark green leaves. Flowers in spring are white
or pinkish, urn shaped; berries are black.

V. parvifolium. Red huckleberry. Deciduous. Zones
5-9. Slow growing, 4 to 12-foot spreading or cascading
plant with intricate, filmy winter silhouette. Thin, light
green, oval leaves are less than an inch long. Greenish
to white flowers develop into showy, clear red berries.
Plant in partial shade.

VIBURNUM

**One-seeded, berrylike fruits eaten by many species;
a particular favorite of bluebirds, waxwings, cardinals,
black-headed and pine grosbeaks, mockingbirds, robins, white-throated and song sparrows, starlings, hermit thrushes, brown towhees.**

Deciduous and evergreen shrubs. Most viburnums are
especially attractive landscape shrubs. Many are notable for their spring show of small flowers in large
clusters; for their good looking foliage; for their abundant crop of bright, berrylike fruits; or for their brilliant autumn foliage. Many combine several or all of
these features. Most will take either acid or alkaline
soil, and prefer a good soil with abundant moisture.
They will grow in sun or shade, although the evergreen

kinds look better with some protection from sun where
summers are hot and long. There are countless viburnum species and named varieties sold, almost any of
which will attract birds if they bear fruit. Exceptions
are the "snowball" types, the flowers of which are
sterile and never bear fruit. From the many different
viburnums sold, here are some of the most popular.

V. bitchiuense. Deciduous. Zones 7-10. Grows to 10
feet high. Has oval, downy leaves to 3½ inches long.
Mid-spring, pinkish flowers fading to white are especially fragrant; blue-black fruits follow. Autumn foliage is dull red.

V. burkwoodii. Burkwood viburnum. Deciduous in
coldest areas, nearly evergreen where winters are mild.
Zones 5-10. Dark green leaves (to 3½ inches long) are
glossy above but white and hairy beneath; they turn
red to purplish in autumn cold. Dense 4-inch clusters
of white flowers appear in very early spring; black fruits
ripen in late summer. Mature plants are dense, 6 to 12
feet tall, and a little more than half as wide.

V. carlesii. Korean spice viburnum. Deciduous. Zones
5-10. Small clusters of white flowers in early spring are
sweetly fragrant; early summer fruits are black. Grows
4 to 8 feet tall, nearly as wide, with dull green leaves
that turn reddish purple in fall.

V. cassinoides. Withe rod. Deciduous. Zones 3-9. Six-
foot shrub, rather upright and compact, also adaptable
to planting in masses to form a thicket. Shiny, oval,
yellow-green leaves turn red in autumn. Tiny white
flowers form 3 to 4-inch clusters in late spring, then
form small fruits that ripen in late summer after going
through several color changes: green to yellowish to
red to black, often with all colors in a single cluster.

V. davidii. David viburnum. Evergreen. Zones 7-10. Unusually neat and polished small plant useful in foreground plantings. Only 1 to 3 feet tall and 3 to 4 feet
wide; it has handsome, oval, 3 to 6-inch-long leaves
that are leathery, glossy dark green with three prominent veins running their length. Three-inch clusters of

Viburnum plicatum tomentosum (*Doublefile viburnum*)
offers showy flower display before the berries form.

tiny white flowers are not showy, but fruits in early autumn are an attractive metallic turquoise blue. Set out more than one plant for abundant berry production.

V. dentatum. Arrowwood. Deciduous. Zones 3-9. Fifteen-foot plant with many stems rising from the ground; best used as background plant or for mass effect. Single plants are not as attractive as many other viburnums. White flower clusters in mid-spring are followed by blue berries in fall, at which time the glossy green, sharply toothed leaves turn red.

V. dilatatum. Linden viburnum. Deciduous. Zones 6-9. Tall, broad, and compact — to about 10 feet high and wide. Leaves are nearly round, 2 to 5 inches long and strongly veined; autumn color is red. In mid-spring an abundance of creamy white flowers appear in flat, 5-inch clusters; very showy red berries ripen in autumn and hang on into winter.

V. farreri. Fragrant viburnum. Sometimes sold as *V. fragrans.* Deciduous. Zones 7-10. Fragrant white flowers in 2-inch clusters open from pink buds before plant leafs out in spring. In coldest areas, buds often come too early and may be frozen — therefore eliminating any red to black fruits for that year. In mild-winter regions it may bloom in winter. The 2 to 3-inch, oval leaves are heavily veined, turning bronzy red in fall. An upright, 10-foot shrub, spreading nearly as wide.

V. juddii. Judd viburnum. Deciduous. Zones 5-10. A hybrid with *V. carlesii* as one parent and similar to the parent but more spreading and bushy.

V. lantana. Wayfaring tree. Deciduous. Zones 4-9. Large shrub or even small tree to 15 feet tall; has unusual ability to grow well in dry soils. Broadly oval leaves (to 5 inches long) are downy on both sides; turn red in fall. Tiny white flowers in 2 to 4-inch clusters form small fruits that turn red in autumn, then blacken and shrivel like raisins — hanging on into winter.

V. lentago. Nannyberry. Deciduous. Zones 3-9. For the large or "wild" garden, a dense background shrub to 30 feet high. Autumn foliage is purplish red; black berries in winter.

V. odoratissimum. Sweet viburnum. Evergreen. Zones 8-10. Handsome bright green leaves 3 to 8 inches long with a glossy, varnished looking surface. Grows to 10 feet or more tall, spreading wider. White flowers are in 3 to 6-inch conical clusters; red fruit ripens black in autumn.

V. opulus. European cranberry bush. Deciduous. Zones 4-10. Vigorous, dense plant to over 10 feet high. Leaves (2 to 4 inches long) are lobed like some maples; turn red in autumn. Clusters of small, fertile, white flowers are surrounded by a ring of showy sterile flowers nearly an inch across. Brilliant red berries remain on the plant into winter, after leaves have fallen.

V. plicatum tomentosum. Doublefile viburnum. Deciduous. Zones 5-10. To 15 feet tall and as wide, with distinctive horizontal branching pattern. Strongly veined, oval leaves are dull dark green (to 6 inches long), turn purplish red in fall. Flat, 2 to 4-inch clusters of fertile white flowers are ringed by inch-wide, sterile flowers; the fertile flowers produce showy bright red fruits in autumn. Flower and fruit clusters carried on upper sides of branches. The variety 'Mariesii' has larger, sterile flowers.

V. rhytidophyllum. Leatherleaf viburnum. Evergreen. Zones 6-10. Narrow, upright plant 6 to 15 feet tall, especially noticeable because of its narrow, 4 to 10-inch leaves that are deep green and wrinkled on the upper surface, densely fuzzy underneath. Off-white flowers come in clusters 4 to 8 inches across, followed by fruits that turn from red to black as they ripen.

V. sargentii. Sargent cranberry bush. Deciduous. Zones 5-9. Generally similar to *V. opulus,* but a somewhat stronger growing, larger species.

V. sieboldii. Siebold viburnum. Deciduous. Zones 5-9. Good looking for the background planting, the large garden, or as a single specimen if you have the room. Grows to 20 feet or more, upright and full. Dark green, oval 6-inch leaves turn red in fall. Cream-white flowers are in 5-inch clusters, producing summer fruits that change from red to black as they ripen, each berry on a short red stem in the cluster.

V. tinus. Laurustinus. Evergreen. Zones 7-10. Neat, dense plant 6 to 12 feet high and half as wide. Relatively narrow growth makes it suitable for an unclipped hedge or barrier planting. Leaves are dark green, oval and leathery, 2 to 3 inches long. New stems are wine-red. Small clusters of pink buds open from autumn through spring into white flowers; metallic blue fruits follow, lasting through summer.

V. trilobum. American cranberry bush. Deciduous. Zones 3-9. Similar in all respects to *V. opulus,* but has slightly more open growth and will take colder winters. Red fruits are edible.

V. wrightii. Wright viburnum. Deciduous. Zones 7-9. Narrow, erect shrub 6 to 10 feet tall with showy bright red fruits from late summer into winter. Oval leaves are smooth, bright green, and 2 to 5 inches long.

WEIGELA

Funnel-shaped flowers in late spring lure hummingbirds; red-flowered plants are favored.

Deciduous shrubs. Zone 6 (sometimes 5-9). Coarse-leafed, stiff and rather rangy plants best used where flowers can be enjoyed during spring but where the plants won't be on display during the rest of the year. Funnel-shaped flowers form singly or in short clusters along previous season's branches. After bloom, prune branches that have flowered back to unflowered side branches, cut out some of the oldest stems completely, and thin new shoots from the ground to a few of the most vigorous. Many named hybrids are sold, generally 6 to 10 feet tall. Flowers may be white, pink, rose-red, or bright red. A shorter shrub (3 to 4 feet) with yellow, inch-long flowers, is *W. middendorffiana.*

FOR DESERT DWELLERS ONLY...

If you live in the desert, you may want to plant (or already have) desert plants in your garden. Many of these plants will attract birds. In fact, some are intimately associated with birds found nowhere else but in the desert. The following list doesn't include all such plants, but it does single out some of the most familiar — along with why each is appreciated by birds.

CARNEGIEA gigantea. Saguaro. A giant cactus, columnar and branching, to about 50 feet (but slow growing). Offers housing and food to wide range of desert birds. In May, ash-throated flycatchers, gilded flickers, and other birds eat the large white flowers. Fruits that follow are popular with white-winged doves, mourning doves, cactus wrens, curve-billed thrashers, Gila woodpeckers, and gilded flickers. Small cavities left in saguaros by woodpeckers make good nesting spots for elf owls.

CELTIS pallida. Western hackberry. A 25 to 30-foot-high and as wide deciduous tree with oval, 4-inch-long leaves on somewhat pendulous branches. Berries produced during summer attract finches, Gambel's quail, Bendire's thrashers, curve-billed thrashers, mockingbirds, and white-winged doves. Many birds find excellent nesting sites.

CERCIDIUM floridum, C. microphyllum. Blue palo verde and Littleleaf palo verde, respectively. Fast growing deciduous trees to 25 feet high and as wide; both have spiny branches, tiny leaflets, and a blanket of small yellow flowers in spring. Hummingbirds and verdins are attracted to the flowers, insects are eaten by finches, mockingbirds, and other desert birds. Dense twig and branch structure offers good nesting sites.

CHILOPSIS linearis. Desert willow. An open and airy, large deciduous shrub or small tree with long, willowlike leaves. Hummingbirds and verdins feed on the trumpet-shaped blossoms that appear in spring and sometimes fall.

CITRUS. Oranges, tangerines, grapefruits, lemons, limes. Dense, large shrubs or small trees with polished green, oval leaves up to 5 inches long. Hummingbirds enjoy the flowers, but other desert birds have made use of the fruit of some. From November to May, when citrus fruit has sweetened and other food sources are unavailable, curve-billed thrashers and Gila woodpeckers pierce the tough skins with their strong beaks and eat the fruit through these holes.

ECHINOCACTUS. Barrel cactus; common names vary with different species. Spiny, barrel-shaped cactus that grows slowly to about 4 feet high. Flowers in April and May turn into coarse yellow fruits filled with seeds. The curve-billed thrash-ers, Gila woodpeckers, and gilded flickers will penetrate the fruits to eat seeds.

FOUQUIERIA splendens. Ocotillo. A "shrub" of upright, whiplike gray stems 8 to 25 feet high, heavily furrowed and covered with stout thorns. Foot-long clusters of tubular red flowers appear after rains in summer, attracting hummingbirds.

OLEA europaea. Olive. Evergreen tree. Can be trained to a single trunk but usually seen as multi-trunked tree becoming gnarled and picturesque with age. Gray-green, willowlike foliage, gray branches and trunks. Ultimate size is 25 to 30 feet high and as wide; young plants put on height moderately fast, but bulk takes time. Black, bitter fruits can be messy on pavement, but are favored by curve-billed thrashers, mockingbirds, robins, tanagers, and waxwings.

OPUNTIA. Prickly pear, Cholla cactuses; common names vary with different species. Although definitions are rather loose, those having flat, rather oval segments are "prickly pears"; those with cylindrical segments are "chollas." Spiny, multi-branched plants up to 15 feet tall in the largest species. They provide nesting sites for cactus wrens, curve-billed thrashers, desert roadrunners, mourning doves, and sparrows.

PALMS (many different species). Any palm allowed to retain its old, dead fronds in a thatch along the trunk provides nesting opportunities for house finches, house sparrows, and mourning doves. Gila woodpeckers and gilded flickers find insects among the fronds and in the bark.

PHOENIX dactylifera. Date palm. Although not native to the desert, the date palm is a familiar plant in the warmer winter regions. Dates provide food for cardinals, curve-billed thrashers, and house finches.

PROSOPIS glandulosa torreyana. Mesquite. Wide spreading, deciduous shade tree to 30 feet tall with many tiny green leaflets all through the thicketlike crown. Provides nesting places for mourning doves, white-winged doves, verdins, and phainopeplas. Many insects living in mesquite attract insect-eating birds.

PUNICA granatum. Pomegranate. Deciduous 10-foot shrub or small tree; not a desert native but food for some desert birds. Tolerates great heat and strongly alkaline soil. Narrow, glossy leaves; showy orange flowers and apple-size dull red fruit. When fruits mature in September and October, they often crack open (especially if plants are watered deeply after a long drought); seeds inside eaten by cardinals, curve-billed thrashers, Gila woodpeckers, gilded flickers, house finches, and house sparrows.

Vines and Ground Covers

AMPELOPSIS brevipedunculata. BLUEBERRY CLIMBER

Berries favored by wood thrushes, common flickers, gray catbirds, eastern bluebirds, brown thrashers, bobwhites.

Deciduous vines. Zones 5-10. Strong, rampant climber to 20 feet, but its twining tendrils need a support to wrap themselves around in order to climb. Dark green leaves (to 5 inches wide) are three-lobed; in mild climates they turn red and drop in autumn, but new leaves continue to come out, then change color all winter. Many clusters of small, grapelike berries turn from greenish ivory to brilliant metallic blue in late summer and fall. Grows easily in sun or shade.

ARCTOSTAPHYLOS uva-ursi. BEARBERRY OR
KINNIKINNICK

Relatively tasteless fruits supplement diet of fox sparrows, solitaires, California quail, 30 other bird species. Hummingbirds enjoy nectar from spring flowers.

Evergreen ground cover. Zones 3-10. Native to both coasts of United States as well as northern states. Prostrate and spreading to about 15 feet, but rooting as it creeps so that one plant usually becomes many. Bright, glossy green and leathery leaves are no more than an inch long; they turn red in winter. White or pinkish, urn-shaped flowers produce small pink to bright red berries. Needs moist soil to establish itself, but otherwise gets along well with little moisture in poor or sandy soils where little else will grow. In such situations, however, it must have a cool summer or coastal climate.

BERCHEMIA scandens. SUPPLEJACK

Clusters of blue-black, small fruit eaten by hermit thrushes, brown thrashers, robins, mockingbirds, bobwhites, gray catbirds.

Deciduous vine. Zones 7-10. Woodland native of southeastern states. In the garden it reaches 15 to 20 feet; oblong leaves to 2 inches have distinctive parallel veins. Inconspicuous flowers are followed by clusters of small, blue-black fruits.

CELASTRUS scandens. AMERICAN BITTERSWEET

Often chosen for nesting sites. Fruits, ripening in late fall and winter, eaten by eastern bluebirds, cardinals, gray catbirds, pine grosbeaks, robins, mockingbirds, house sparrows, cedar waxwings, starlings.

Deciduous vine. Zones 3-9. Climbing by twining its branches, this vigorous, 20-foot vine may actually strangle shrubs or small trees if it gets a foothold in them. Light green, oval, toothed leaves are 4 to 5 inches long, turning yellow in fall. Flowers are not noticeable. Because male and female blooms are borne on separate plants, you will need both to get colorful fall fruits. The yellow fruit capsules later split open to reveal red seeds.

COCCULUS carolinus. CAROLINA SNAILSEED

Fruits eaten by eastern bluebirds, mockingbirds, robins, phoebes, brown thrashers.

Deciduous vine. Zones 7-9. Restrained, twining growth reaches 6 to 12 feet. Leaves vary from nearly round to almost triangular, sometimes slightly lobed, 3 to 4 inches long. Flowers are not showy but they ripen in summer to form clusters of red fruits, each less than an inch long. Both male and female plants are needed for fruit set. Prefers moist soils.

CORNUS canadensis. BUNCHBERRY

Pine grosbeaks and bobwhites frequently eat bright red fruits.

Deciduous ground cover. Zones 3-7. Creeping root stocks send up 6 to 9-inch-high stems topped by a whorl of four to six oval or rounding leaves. Each leaf is 1 to 2 inches long and deep rich green, turning yellow in fall. The plant is a perennial rather than shrub, dying down to the ground in winter. Flowers, surrounded by

Cornus canadensis (Bunchberry) is ground-level relative of large dogwoods, produces bright-red fruits.

. . . *Cornus canadensis (cont'd.)*

small white bracts, appear in late spring; clusters of small, shiny, bright red fruits are produced in early fall. Prefers cool, moist climates and acid soil.

COTONEASTER

Favored by hummingbirds for spring flowers. Showy red berries draw bluebirds, robins, fox sparrows, cedar waxwings, purple finches, mockingbirds, thrushes.

Deciduous and evergreen ground covers. Low-spreading and prostrate cotoneasters make trouble-free, tough ground covers—most attractive if given room to spread without restriction. Leaves are generally oval and under 1 inch long; flowers are white or pink tinted, and fruits are bright red and showy. Good looking plants in all seasons; even the deciduous species show interesting branch patterns during winter.

C. adpressa. Creeping cotoneaster. Deciduous. Zones 5-10. Slow growing ground cover for small areas; ultimate spread is about 6 feet with height to 1 foot. Dark green, ½-inch leaves. Will follow contours of ground, rocks, and will even drape down a wall. Subspecies *C. a. praecox* has slightly larger leaves and fruits and is a taller (to 1½ feet) more widely spreading plant.

C. conspicua 'Decora.' Necklace cotoneaster. Evergreen. Zones 6-10. Tiny dark green leaves (paler beneath) on an almost prostrate plant. Main stems spread with short, rigid branches growing upward.

C. dammeri. Bearberry cotoneaster. Evergreen. Zones 6-10. Vigorous, long, prostrate branches spread to 10 feet, rooting as they spread. Height is only 3 to 6 inches. One-inch, oval, dark green leaves are glossy on top, whitish beneath. Grows in sun or part shade. Will cascade down a wall, and flow over and around rocks.

C. horizontalis. Rock cotoneaster. Deciduous. Zones 5-10. Spreading to 15 feet, this taller ground cover

grows 2 to 3 feet high. Main branches grow stiffly at angles; secondary branches arch fanlike from them. Rounded, ½-inch leaves are glossy above, pale beneath, and turn orange to red in autumn. Needs room to spread naturally; pruning to confine its growth creates awkward looking plant. Subspecies *C. h. perpusilla* is a lower, more compact grower.

C. 'Lowfast'. Evergreen. Zones 7-9. Very vigorous, fast growing variety (spreads as much as 2 feet per year) with an ultimate spread of 10 to 15 feet, rooting as it goes. Height is about 12 inches. Good bank cover, it will also cascade over a wall.

C. microphylla. Rockspray cotoneaster. Evergreen. Zones 6-10. Many branches spread to 6 feet, rooting along the way; secondary branches grow upright, 2 to 3 feet. Has tiny leaves. The subspecies *C. m. cochleata* is more compact and lower growing, moulding itself to contours of the ground.

C. salicifolia 'Herbstfeuer'. Evergreen to semi-deciduous. Zones 7-10. Grows only 6 inches high but spreads to 8 feet. Leaves are narrow and willowlike up to 3½ inches long, wrinkled dark green above but grayish green beneath.

EMPETRUM nigrum. BLACK CROWBERRY

Dark, berrylike fruits persist throughout winter, attracting pine grosbeaks, robins, waxwings.

Evergreen ground cover. Zones 4-8. Only 2 to 3 feet across and 10 inches high; better suited to rock gardens or confined spaces than for covering large patches of earth. Needs cool, moist, acid soil and cool, moist summers. Numerous, very narrow leaves are only ½ inch long. Tiny, purplish spring flowers develop into black, berrylike autumn fruits.

FRAGARIA. STRAWBERRY

Berries eaten by these birds: robins, grosbeaks, quail, towhees, gray catbirds, thrashers, wood thrushes, 50 other species.

Evergreen ground covers. Decorative assets are shiny dark green leaves, small white blossoms, and red fruits. Birds will eat any of the large edible strawberries; but some varieties grown primarily as foliage ground covers also bear a crop of small fruits for birds.

F. chiloensis. Zones 5-10. Forms low, compact, lush mat 6 to 12 inches high; dark green, glossy leaves have three toothed leaflets that take on red tints in winter. Will cover any area of ground thoroughly if you set plants 12 to 18 inches apart. Unfortunately, little fruit is normally set in gardens. A hybrid of this species and a commercial fruiting variety, called 'Number 25', is generally similar to the species but is taller (to 15 inches) and will bear fruit consistently. Plants should be fertilized in late spring, watered regularly, and mowed or cut back yearly in early spring to prevent stem build-up and force new growth.

F. virginiana. Zones 4-10. A wild strawberry native to eastern states, generally similar to *F. chiloensis* but only 4 to 8 inches high with light green leaves.

GAULTHERIA. WINTERGREEN

Berrylike fruits, ripening in September, favored by bobwhites, brown thrashers, chickadees, purple finches, white and golden-crowned sparrows, thrushes, towhees. Berries can have intoxicating effect on birds eating them.

Evergreen ground covers. An east coast and west coast native are represented here; both have small urn-shaped flowers and red, berrylike fruits. Need moist but well-drained, acid soils with addition of organic matter such as peat moss or leaf mold.

G. ovatifolia. Oregon wintergreen. Zones 6-9. Spreading, trailing plant that also produces upright branches to 8 inches high. Oval, leathery, dark green leaves are up to 1½ inches long and nearly as wide. White to pinkish flowers appear in summer; berries come in fall and winter.

G. procumbens. Wintergreen or Checkerberry. Zones 4-9. Creeps and trails, but upright branches reach only 3 to 6 inches high. Two-inch, oval, glossy leaves are clustered toward branch tips. Tiny white blooms in summer, red berries in fall.

G. shallon. Salal. Zones 7-9. Pacific Coast native shrub ranging from 1 to 10 feet tall, depending upon habitat. Tallest in shade and good, moist soil; short in sun and poor, dry soil. Leaves glossy bright green, broadly ovaled, to 4 inches long. Small, bell-shaped flowers in spring are white or pinkish, in 6-inch-long clusters; black, blueberrylike fruits follow. Needs acid soil.

HEDERA. IVY

Nesting sites for various birds. Robins eat berries of H. helix only when other food is scarce.

Evergreen woody vines. Tough and durable vines (and also ground covers) that cling tenaciously to vertical surfaces. Foliage cover is dense. As stems age they become quite thick and woody. Eventually old plants flower, producing small, black fruits.

H. canariensis. Algerian ivy. Zones 9-10. Shiny, rich green leaves are 5 to 8 inches wide with three to five shallow lobes. Variety 'Variegata' has leaves edged with yellowish white.

H. helix. English ivy. Zones 6-10. Leaves are 2 to 4 inches wide and long with three to five lobes; color is dull dark green veined with a paler green. Variety 'Baltica' is the most cold-tolerant of ivies; leaves turn purplish in winter.

LONICERA. HONEYSUCKLE

Shelter and nesting sites in plants established for several years. Hummingbirds like tubular flowers. Berries attract pine grosbeaks, robins, solitaires, hermit thrushes, gray catbirds, red-eyed vireos, chickadees, finches.

Evergreen and deciduous vines. Some vining honeysuckles are rampant growing and almost weedy; others are more restrained. All need some initial support on which to climb.

L. henryi. Henry honeysuckle. Evergreen to semi-deciduous. Zones 5-10. Nearly one-inch-long flowers are red-tinted yellow or purple, followed by small black fruits. Leaves are narrow, dark green, to 3 inches long on hairy branches.

L. hildebrandiana. Giant Burmese honeysuckle. Evergreen. Zones 9-10. In all respects a big plant, although its size is easily controlled. Supple, ropelike stems carry 4 to 6-inch, oval, highly polished dark green leaves. Fragrant, tubular summer flowers are 6 to 7 inches long, opening white but fading to yellow or orange; inch-wide, dark green berrylike fruits sometimes follow.

L. japonica. Japanese honeysuckle. Vine or ground cover, evergreen to deciduous depending upon severity of winter. Zones 5-10. Variety 'Halliana' (Hall's honeysuckle) is form usually sold. A rank, almost smothering vine with oval, deep green leaves to 3 inches long. Summer flowers are white aging to yellow; autumn fruits are black. May need annual trimming back to main stems to prevent buildup of dead undergrowth.

L. periclymenum. Woodbine. Deciduous vine (or a twining shrub) to 20 feet. Zones 5-10. In summer and fall bears very fragrant, yellowish white flowers that open from purplish red buds, followed by red fruits. Variety 'Belgica', (Dutch woodbine) is even more fragrant, and flowers open from pale purple buds. Dark green leaves are oval, 1½ to 3 inches long; lighter green underneath.

L. sempervirens. Trumpet honeysuckle. Evergreen to semi-deciduous vine. Zones 4-10. Shrubby unless given support on which to climb. Showy but unscented summer blooms are yellow-orange to red, trumpet shaped, up to 2 inches long, produced in whorls at ends of branches. Fruits that follow are red. Oval leaves (to 3 inches long) are blue-green underneath.

LYCIUM halimifolium. MATRIMONY VINE

Fall and winter berries attract robins and other fruit eaters. Provides good shelter, nesting sites.

Deciduous. Zones 5-9. Not strictly a vine or a ground cover, but a rambling, sprawling, thicket-forming shrub. Best used as bank cover where soil is poor and dry; it covers easily by rooting where branches touch ground. In the garden, with reasonable soil and care, it can quickly become an invasive pest. Branches are prickly. Small, orange-red, berrylike fruits appear in fall, following small, pale purple summer flowers.

PARTHENOCISSUS. BOSTON IVY, VIRGINIA CREEPER

Good cover for most birds; good nesting sites for bushtits, house finches. Grapelike berries ripen in fall, attracting eastern bluebirds, gray catbirds, common flickers, eastern kingbirds, mockingbirds, robins, yellow-bellied sapsuckers, brown thrashers, Swainson's thrushes, red-eyed vireos, yellow-rumped warblers, woodpeckers, white-breasted nuthatches, black-capped chickadees.

Deciduous vine. Known for brilliant and dependable orange to red autumn color as well as ability to cling to anything. Overlapping leaves form dense cover or shelter. Not particular about soil as long as it is fairly moist, but best growth comes in better soils.

P. quinquefolia. Virginia creeper. Zones 4-10. Leaves are divided into five separate, elongated 6-inch leaflets with saw-toothed edges. Growth is more open than *P. tricuspidata*. For a smaller-leafed, more dense variety of Virginia creeper, choose the variety 'Engelmannii'. Blue-black, grapelike berries appear in fall.

Parthenocissus tricuspidata (Boston ivy) gives good shelter with overlapping leaves, sturdy stems.

P. tricuspidata. Boston ivy. Zones 5-10. Glossy leaves vary in shape but usually are three-lobed and up to 8 inches wide; varieties 'Lowii' and 'Veitchii' have much smaller leaves and are less rampant. Grows well in city dust and soot. Blue-black berries in fall.

RUBUS. BLACKBERRY, RASPBERRY

Sprawling branchlets offer good nesting sites. Eating various berries are eastern bluebirds, bobwhites, cardinals, gray catbirds, black-headed and pine grosbeaks, mockingbirds, orioles, 100 other species.

Deciduous thicket-forming shrub-vines. Hardiness varies according to species or variety. Includes all cultivated blackberries, raspberries, loganberries, youngberries as well as the wild species (from which they developed) and other wild kinds not usually grown for fruit. Growing commercial varieties for birds can be a waste of time, and in a small garden, growing them in thickets for birds is often a waste of space. Nevertheless, in a "wild" garden (where neatness is not so important) and on rural properties, a thorny thicket of any wild species will offer good shelter and protection, nesting sites, and some food during brief summer season. (If you have no source for wild species, plant a thorny cultivated variety and let it grow wild.) Blackberries are the most aggressive.

SMILAX rotundifolia. GREENBRIER, CATBRIER

Eating fruits are cardinals, gray catbirds, common flickers, mockingbirds, 50 other species. Sprawling stems provide excellent nesting and shelter sites.

Deciduous vine. Zones 5-9. Tough, persistent plant that, once established, is hard to eradicate. Heart-shaped leaves grow to 4½ inches long, glossy green on prickly stems. Black berries appear in fall. Best in the larger or "wild" garden where it can form a large, impenetrable mass.

SYMPHORICARPOS mollis. CREEPING SNOWBERRY

In northwestern states, grosbeaks, robins, thrushes, wrentits, and towhees have been seen eating the berries but only very late in the season when other fruits are gone.

Deciduous ground cover. Zones 7-10. Really a shrub to 18 inches high that will spread widely by underground rootstalks. Fewer flowers and smaller fruits, but otherwise similar to *Symphoricarpos albus* (see page 84), in appearance and color.

TECOMARIA capensis. CAPE HONEYSUCKLE

Hummingbirds flock to bright orange, tubular blossoms.

Evergreen vine or shrub. Zones 8-10. A 25-foot vine if tied to support; a 6 to 8-foot upright shrub if consistently pruned. Leaves divided into many dark, glistening green leaflets. Brilliant orange-red, tubular flowers (to 2 inches long) come in clusters in fall through winter. Withstands sun, heat, wind, salt air, and some drought when established. Needs well-drained soil. Variety 'Aurea' has yellow flowers and lighter green foliage on a plant that is smaller and less showy than the typical species; it also requires more heat to perform well.

VITIS. GRAPE

Fruit of wild grape popular with fruit eaters. Eating grapes of cultivated plant are mockingbirds, towhees, blue jays, cardinals, house finches, robins, quail, variety of other species if other fruits are scarce.

Deciduous vines. Hardiness varies according to species or variety. Wild grapes, ancestors or cousins of the cultivated table and wine grapes. Their use is two-fold: grown in a tangle for cover and nesting, and as a source of food. They could be grown for shelter on an arbor or fence, but for those situations, you might as well grow one of the cultivated varieties and have some fruit for yourself. Any grape is, by nature, a far-reaching vine with ropelike stems (eventually much thicker and rigid) with shredding bark. Leaves are large and rounded to about 6 inches and shallowly lobed to about the same size. They climb by means of twining tendrils that wrap around any convenient support; established vines can take over the crown of a tree in a few years. Require place to climb.

❮❮❮❮❮❮❮❮❮❮❮❮❮❮❮❮❮❮❮❮❮❮❮❮❮❮❮❮❮❮❮❮❮❮

ANNUALS, PERENNIALS, OTHERS

In addition to shrubs, trees, vines, and ground covers, there are many common (and some not-so-common) non-woody flowering plants that also attract birds. The most obvious are those colorful flowers (such as scarlet sage and cardinal flower) that attract hummingbirds during spring and summer blooming seasons. Not as well known are the popular annuals that, if left to go to seed at the end of their blooming season, will feed seed-eating birds. And even though they are not usually encouraged to grow, numerous familiar weeds offer tempting seeds. Below are cultural tips (including several suggested varieties) for annuals, perennials, and other plants that may attract birds.

Annuals. There are three ways to start annuals in your garden: 1) sow seed in well-cultivated open ground in spring after danger of frost has passed and soil temperature has begun to warm; 2) sow seeds in flats using good potting soil, later transplanting young seedlings to the open ground; 3) buy small starter plants from a nursery or other plant suppliers and set them out in your garden.

After planting (or after germination, if you sow seeds in the soil), be sure to keep the soil moist until the plants have become established. Favorite hummingbird plants among annuals are: larkspur, morning glory, and scarlet sage. For seed-eating birds, the following plants produce favored seeds: ageratum, aster, bachelor's buttons, coreopsis, cosmos, forget-me-not, marigold, nasturtium, sunflower, and zinnia.

Perennials. Among the perennials (those plants that flower year after year from the same roots) there are many that attract hummingbirds. Cultural directions for these plants vary greatly; but in general they require well-prepared soil (since they remain planted for several years) and periodic dividing, usually after their flowering season. Spring flowering perennials are: aloe, columbine (*Aquilegia*), coral bells (*Heuchera*), foxglove (*Digitalis*), penstemon, and phlox. For summer flowers: bee balm (*Monarda*), busy Lizzie (*Impatiens*), California fuchsia (*Zauschneria*), cardinal flower (*Lobelia cardinalis*), delphinium, hollyhock (*Althaea*), monkey flower (*Mimulus*), tree tobacco (*Nicotiana*), and poker plant (*Kniphofia*). In addition to their flowers attracting hummingbirds, two familiar perennials produce seed for seed-eating birds: California poppy (*Eschscholzia*) and goldenrod (*Solidago*).

Other plants. Weeds, the bane of a gardener's existence, may be looked upon with favor by birds. Some particular weed seeds are especially prized by seed-eating birds. If you have the space to encourage the weeds, some birds may eat the seeds of these plants: dandelion, dock, fennel, plantain, thistle, and any wild grasses and grains.

❮❮❮❮❮❮❮❮❮❮❮❮❮❮❮❮❮❮❮❮❮❮❮❮❮❮❮❮❮❮❮❮❮❮

Suggested Reading List

Bent, Arthur C. *Life Histories of North American Birds* (21 volumes with different titles). Washington: Smithsonian Institution Press (U. S. National Museum), 1919-1968 (reprinted in paperback by Dover Publications). The most comprehensive study, by far, on North American birds.

Davison, Verne E. *Attracting Birds: from the Prairies to the Atlantic*. New York: Thomas Y. Crowell, 1967. Detailed lists of birds (and what they eat) as well as plants (and how birds use them).

Godfrey, W. Earl. *The Birds of Canada*. Ottawa: National Museum of Canada, 1966. Detailed descriptions of birds frequenting Canada.

Martin, Alexander C., H. S. Zim, and A. Nelson. *American Wildlife and Plants*. New York: McGraw-Hill, 1951 (paperback version by Dover Publications). A guide to food habits of birds and mammals, prepared under direction of U. S. Fish and Wildlife Service.

McKenny, Margaret. *Birds in the Garden and How to Attract Them*. New York: Reynal and Hitchcock, 1939. A classic book on familiar birds and native plantings that will attract them.

Pearson, T. Gilbert. *Birds of America*. New York: Garden City Publishing Co., 1936. Good all-round reference for birds and their habits.

Peterson, Roger Tory. *A Field Guide to the Birds* (2nd edition). Boston: Houghton Mifflin, 1947. Standard guide for identifying birds east of the Rockies.

Peterson, Roger Tory. *A Field Guide to Western Birds* (2nd edition). Boston: Houghton Mifflin, 1961. The western counterpart to the above guide (including a section on Hawaiian birds).

Rand, Austin L. *Ornithology: An Introduction*. New York: W. W. Norton and Co., Inc., 1967. Excellent general introduction to birds — from physiology to behavior.

Robbins, Chandler S., Bertel Bruun, and Herbert Zim. *Birds of North America*. New York: Golden Press, 1966. Concise one-volume book for all North American birds, with handy range maps.

Stefferud, Alfred. *Birds in Our Lives*. Washington: U. S. Bureau of Sport Fisheries and Wildlife, Dept. of the Interior, 1966. Over fifty essays view birds — as they relate to man — from differing perspectives.

Terres, John K. *Songbirds in Your Garden*. New York: Crowell, 1968. Enjoyable firsthand accounts of an experienced bird watcher (and attractor).

Vessel, Matthew F. and Herbert H. Wong. *Introducing Our Eastern Birds*. Palo Alto, Calif.: Fearon, 1970. A beginner's guide to the most common eastern birds of home gardens, parks, and roadsides.

Vessel, Matthew F. and Herbert H. Wong. *Introducing Our Western Birds*. Palo Alto, Calif.: Fearon, 1970. The western counterpart to the above guide.

Welty, Joel C. *The Life of Birds*. New York: Alfred H. Knopf, 1963. Begins with chapter on birds as "flying machines" and continues with principles of bird biology with the general audience, not the specialist, in mind.

Wetmore, Alexander, and others. *Song and Garden Birds of North America*. Washington: National Geographic Society, 1964. Covers 327 species and includes a record of songs of 70 species.

Wyman, Donald. *Wyman's Gardening Encyclopedia*. New York: MacMillan Co., 1971. A reference for plants across the United States.

Other sources of help:

In your area, you can get further information on birds and plants from government and state agencies, commercial nurseries, and local bird societies. *The National Audubon Society*, 950 Third Avenue, New York, New York, 10022, is a good central source of information.

Index

Photographers

William Aplin: 54, 65. **Bob and Elsie Boggs:** 50. **Mimi Brandes:** 59. **Christy Brindle:** 84. **Richard Dawson:** 57. **Roger Flanagan:** 79. **Les Flowers, Jr.:** 38, 43 left. **Gerald R. Fredrick:** 39, 43 right, 48, 49, 77. **Art Hupy:** 42 left. **Ells Marugg:** 46, 47 top left, 86. **Don Normark:** 40, 44, 45, 63, 68, 69, 75, 81, 90, 92. **Norman A. Plate:** 56. **Darrow M. Watt:** 42 right, 47 bottom right.